DATE RAPE

Other Books in the At Issue Series:

DATE RAPE

David Bender, *Publisher*
Bruno Leone, *Executive Editor*

Brenda Stalcup, *Managing Editor*
Scott Barbour, *Series Editor*

Mary E. Williams, *Book Editor*

An Opposing Viewpoints® Series

Greenhaven Press, Inc.
San Diego, California

Library of Congress Cataloging-in-Publication Data

Date rape / Mary E. Williams, book editor.
    p.   cm. — (At issue)
    Includes bibliographical references and index.
    ISBN 1-56510-699-7. — ISBN 1-56510-698-9 (pbk.)
    1. Acquaintance rape—United States. 2. Dating violence—United States. I. Williams, Mary E., 1960– . II. Series: At issue (San Diego, Calif.)
HV6561.D36   1998
362.883—dc21   97-36933
                                                                CIP

© 1998 by Greenhaven Press, Inc., PO Box 289009,
San Diego, CA 92198-9009

Printed in the U.S.A.

Table of Contents

Introduction

For many people, the definition of rape remains a violent assault perpetrated by a stranger. Several recent studies on sexual violence, however, conclude that the majority of rapes are committed by a person the victim already knows. According to the 1994 National Health and Social Life Survey conducted by the National Opinion Research Center, 22 percent of rape victims claim that their assailant was someone they knew well, while another 50 percent report that their assailant was someone they were intimate with. The American Medical Association points out that more than 80 percent of college women who claim to have been sexually assaulted report knowing their assailant. "Acquaintance rape" and "date rape" are the terms commonly used to differentiate such assaults from those committed by strangers. But the use of these terms has stirred up controversy among researchers, activists, and criminologists who disagree over the definitions of and the distinction between rape and consensual sex.

Some contend that the popular use of the phrase "date rape" wrongly implies that sexual attacks by acquaintances or partners are less serious and less harmful than assaults by strangers. Former New York City prosecutor Alice Vachss, for example, points out that while most people believe that stranger-to-stranger rape is a crime, acquaintance rape is relegated to a "gray area" of less-injurious conduct that does not require assailants to face significant punishment. In her opinion, the perception that rape by acquaintances is not a serious form of assault reveals society's disrespect for a woman's right to say no to unwanted sex. To disregard this right to say no—even if the woman has willingly engaged in some physical contact—is to commit sexual violence, Vachss maintains. Lois Copeland and Leslie R. Wolfe, authors of *Violence Against Women,* agree, adding that the prevailing definition of "real rape" as a crime committed by a violent stranger harms women and limits society's ability to confront sexual violence: "Acquaintance rape . . . is still defined as a woman's personal problem. The myth that rape is [only] a crime of sexually aroused and violent strangers—not 'normal' men, not friends or dates or partners—further punishes women." Such myths about rape, Copeland and Wolfe maintain, stem from a double standard in which men are expected to be sexually aggressive while women are blamed for "inviting" rape by wearing revealing clothes, flirting, going to bars, or attending campus fraternity parties. Furthermore, the authors point out, the existence of any previous relationship between a rape victim and her assailant suggests, in society's view, that the sex was consensual. "Men who know their victims are least likely to be arrested, prosecuted, and convicted. Where there is so-called 'contributory behavior' by the woman, juries are less likely to convict," assert Copeland and Wolfe. As a result of this sexual double standard, experts maintain, women are discouraged from accusing acquaintance rapists of crimes. Many contend, therefore, that date rape is underreported and rarely convicted.

Several researchers have conducted surveys in an attempt to prove that rape is underreported and to arrive at more accurate statistics on the prevalence of sexual violence. In 1982, psychiatrist and researcher Mary P. Koss was commissioned by *Ms.* magazine to direct a nationwide survey to determine the incidence of rape on college campuses. The three-year study, which was administered to 6,159 students throughout the United States, concluded that "25 percent of women in college have been the victims of rape or attempted rape." In another widely cited 1970s study, researcher Diana E.H. Russell interviewed a random sample of 930 San Francisco women about their lifetime experiences with physical and sexual violence. The results of this study led Russell to claim that "at least 46 percent of American women will be victims of rape or attempted rape at some time in their lives." Moreover, these researchers reiterate, most incidents of sexual violence against women are perpetrated by partners, relatives, or acquaintances of the victim.

In response to the conclusions drawn by Koss, Russell, and other researchers and the claims that accusations of acquaintance rape are often discounted, many individuals and organizations have become involved in social activism and education in an effort to reduce the threat of rape. In the early 1990s, for example, activists on many college campuses initiated various antirape programs, including required sexual assault education for men and women, and rape awareness and prevention workshops. They also funded rape-crisis centers, outlined sexual consent policies, and formed campus grievance boards to conduct hearings concerning accusations of rape. Antioch College in Yellow Springs, Ohio, drew national attention after its sexual-offense policy went into effect in June 1992. The policy, which declares that sexual partners must obtain verbal consent "with each new level of physical and/or sexual contact," explains the different degrees of sexual violation and details the rights of accusers and those accused of rape. Supporters of the Antioch policy contend that it forces students to think more clearly about how they relate sexually to others, thereby decreasing the incidence of sexual assault. Critics, however, argue that such policies are a response to dangerously broad definitions of rape and inflated statistics on the prevalence of rape.

One such critic, University of California professor Neil Gilbert, charges that many of the widely cited rape researchers fail to distinguish between rape and a bad but consensual sexual experience. He disputes Mary P. Koss's contention that one out of four college women are victims of actual or attempted rape because "there is a notable discrepancy between [her] definition of rape and the way most of the women she labeled as victims interpreted their experiences." According to Gilbert, three-quarters of the women Koss defined as rape victims did not believe that they had been raped; moreover, he points out, 42 percent of these women had sex again with the alleged rapist. Gilbert maintains that Koss's definition of rape did not take into account whether the woman expressed lack of consent. He claims, for example, that a "yes" answer to the survey question "Have you had a man attempt sexual intercourse . . . when you didn't want to because a man gave you alcohol or drugs?" does not indicate whether force or the threat of force was present. In Gilbert's opinion, a positive response to such a question "could conceivably mean . . . that a few drinks lowered the respondent's inhibitions and she consented to an act she later regretted." Such a situation does not constitute rape, Gilbert argues.

Gilbert and other critics contend, moreover, that much of the antirape activism seen on campuses—as well as the research claiming an alarmingly high incidence of date rape—is overly influenced by feminist politics. According to Katie Roiphe, author of *The Morning After: Sex, Fear, and Feminism on Campus,* much campus antirape activism is the result of a feminist-promoted belief that rape can result from verbal and emotional pressure on the part of the assailant. In Roiphe's opinion, defining date rape as an outcome of emotional manipulation suggests that rape can occur even when consent is given: "If verbal coercion constitutes rape, then the word rape itself expands to include any kind of sex a woman experiences as negative." Such a definition of rape increases the chances that women will make unwarranted accusations of rape, Roiphe contends. Furthermore, she maintains, claiming that verbal coercion can lead to rape actually demeans women by implying that they are weak-willed, unable to make mature decisions, and defenseless. Roiphe, Gilbert, and others who believe that the threat of date rape has been exaggerated argue, in the end, that broad definitions of rape undermine the credibility of women who actually have been forcibly raped. To prevent further trivialization of the problem of sexual violence, these commentators assert, rape must be defined as unwanted sex that results from physical force or threat of injury.

Whether the definition of rape can be so straightforwardly defined remains controversial, however. In a 1994 *Harper's Magazine* essay, Mary Gaitskill, author of the novel *Two Girls, Fat and Thin,* contends that women can suffer emotional wounds from sexual violations even if those violations cannot legitimately be defined as rape. She recounts her own experience of sexual violation as a teenager, when she had unwanted intercourse under the influence of drugs. Because Gaitskill did not communicate her lack of consent, she does not define the incident as a rape. However, she explains, "I [had] let myself be drawn into sex because I could not face the idea that if I said no, things might get ugly." Gaitskill felt seriously violated by the incident and only as an adult was able to understand that "I was unable to stand up for myself because I had never been taught how." In her opinion, arriving at a universally agreed upon definition of date rape should not be the focal point of efforts to reduce sexual assault. Instead, she argues, society should concentrate on educating girls and women to think and stand up for themselves.

The question of how to define rape continues to be a subject of debate among academics, researchers, and activists. The authors in *At Issue: Date Rape* offer a wide array of opinions on the extent of date rape and the effectiveness of various responses to the problem.

1

Date Rape Is a Form of Sexual Violence

Julie A. Allison and Lawrence S. Wrightsman

Julie A. Allison, a researcher in the area of rape and sexual aggression, is a professor of social psychology at Pittsburg State University in Pittsburg, Kansas. Lawrence S. Wrightsman is a legal-system researcher who specializes in eyewitness identification and jury selection. He is also a psychology professor at the University of Kansas in Lawrence, Kansas. Allison and Wrightsman are the authors of Rape: The Misunderstood Crime, *from which the following viewpoint is excerpted.*

In most cases, rape is committed by a person the victim knows. Since societal attitudes dictate that women should be responsible for maintaining sexual boundaries in male/female relationships, women are often blamed for their own victimization and the serious consequences of acquaintance rape are often unacknowledged. But the fact that the assailant and the victim know each other does not diminish the severity of a sexual assault. Victims of acquaintance and date rape frequently blame themselves for the attack and are therefore less likely than victims of stranger rape to seek help in recovering from the trauma. Because date-rape victims do not often pursue therapy, they may experience more psychological distress than do victims of stranger rape.

Almost everyone is aware of the encounter between Jessica Hahn and television evangelist Jim Bakker. Although each portrays their sexual interaction somewhat differently, they both acknowledge that it did happen and that their assignation had been arranged by a mutual acquaintance. Ms. Hahn describes herself as naive when it happened; an ever-trusting follower of the evangelical minister, she was overcome by Jim Bakker's approach when they met for the first time in a motel room reserved for her in Florida.

And although everyone is aware of what happened, to call it *acquaintance rape* may be a surprise to some. But if we accept Ms. Hahn's description of the details of the meeting, that is just what it was. Ms. Hahn knew of Mr. Bakker; she had watched his program and contributed money to his cause. In that sense they were not strangers. And according to her account, he forced himself upon her; she tried to resist but succumbed. The result was a rape. Furthermore, it was, she reports, her first sexual encounter; "I will never in my life know what it's like to make love for the first time with a man I love" (Goodman, 1987, p. 5A).

The incidence of date rape and acquaintance rape

What most people fail to realize is that most rapes involve people who are acquainted with each other. It happens off campus as well as on; the victim could be a 50-year-old woman who asked the man next door to repair her toaster, or a single 35-year-old office worker who got a ride home with a colleague (Lewin, 1991). Such types of rape—known as acquaintance rape or date rape, depending on the circumstances—have been around for a long time; the Old Testament (2 Sam. 13: 1–15) describes an acquaintance rape committed by Amnon, son of King David. But only recently have they come to receive attention by both the mass media and researchers in the social sciences. (The term *date rape* was apparently first used in a September, 1982, article in *Ms.* magazine.)

To be raped by someone you know—someone who knows he is known and recognized—is not an irrational abstraction or a figment of a woman's imagination. It happens, and the fact that the rapist is familiar to the victim makes it no less ugly or repugnant. The fact that some victims of such assaults had taken drugs or had one drink too many likewise does not mitigate the seriousness of the act. A rape is a rape and its consequences cannot be trivialized just because of some prior expectations by the woman or prior relationship with the assailant. Yet some date rapists—and sometimes society in general—may treat it as a different phenomenon. For example, D. Richardson and J.L. Campbell (1982) found that a rapist was blamed less for an assault when he was intoxicated than when he was sober. Also see Box 1.

It is difficult to estimate how many date rapes and acquaintance rapes occur. Many, if not most, of the rapes of this type are never reported to any governmental or social agency; Mary P. Koss (1985) found that only 5% of victims reported the assault to the police. Even estimating the incidence has its problems; to do so, researchers are forced to rely on questionnaires that ask women about their experiences with sexual aggression, and women sometimes do not label themselves as "rape victims" when the instigator is an acquaintance (Koss, 1985). Despite these limitations, Koss found that 15% of the college women she surveyed described experiences that would fulfill legal definitions of rape. Andrea Parrot's survey of two campuses concluded that 20% of the women had been forced into sex (Leo, 1987), and C.L. Muehlenhard and S.W. Cook's (1988) survey reported 11% of college women had engaged in unwanted sexual intercourse because the other person got them drunk and took advantage of the situation.

Many women, thinking back on their sexual experiences, will respond affirmatively when asked the question "Have you ever had sex with a man when you didn't want to, because he used physical force against you?" but at the same time offer a firm "no" when asked "Have you ever been raped?" In one study, in every incidence of this combination, the woman knew the rapist (Muehlenhard, 1988). However, even though victims may not label the experience as rape per se, they suffer similar psychological and physical consequences as those self-acknowledged rape victims. Koss (1988a) has reported, for example, that measures were taken 2 years before the year of the rape and 2 years following that year (5 years total). Victims were seeking general medical treatment (not directly related to the rape) up to 2 years following the year that the rape occurred.

Box 1: Date Rape: An Extreme View

Despite the recent publicity about date rape, dissenters and disbelievers still exist. A letter to Ann Landers:

Dear Ann: If I read one more letter in your column from a woman who says she was date raped I may cancel my subscription to the paper.

Date rape is 20-20 hindsight fiction, invented by easy sluts posing as hard-to-get and "virtuous."

Any girl whose vocal chords are intact can scream her head off while kicking, scratching, squirming, and seeking a way to escape.

Before you believe her claim of date rape, ask if all four of her limbs were immobilized, her mouth gagged and her hips held in a vise-like grip?

Also ask her why she didn't kick him in the most vulnerable spot, which would have been easy to do if she had wanted to.

If you get a believable answer, please share it with your readers instead of insulting their intelligence by printing such clap-trap.—Proud to be a Pig. (Landers, 1988, p. 5A; permission granted by Ann Landers and Creators Syndicate)

Several explanations exist concerning why these women refuse to acknowledge that they have been raped, even though the act and the circumstance qualify it for a legal definition of rape. Some women simply may not believe that they were raped. How can you be raped, they may ask themselves, by someone you know and trust? As one woman who was raped by a "friend" explains in a letter she wrote to Ann Landers, "It took several days before I realized I was raped. Things get muddled and emotions get scrambled" (Landers, 1987). In addition, admitting to yourself that you have been raped necessarily means conceding the fact that you have been a "victim"—a very vulnerable place to find yourself.

Researchers sometimes have taken this latter aspect into consideration by administering questions that deal with rape as it is legally defined without actually including the dreaded word. As recently as 1988 the best estimates suggested that about one half of all rapes occurred between acquaintances or dates. But more recent estimates suggest that in *most* rapes the victim and her assailant were familiar to each other. One of the most

Box 2: Three Types of Date Relationships

R. Lance Shotland (1989) has proposed that different processes may lead to a rape at different points in a relationship's development. In doing so, he offered an explanation for the inconsistencies in explanations for the causes of date rape—for example, the contrast between an explanation focusing on the psychopathology of violent behavior and one that emphasizes traditional processes in courtship.

Shotland proposes that "date rape can be separated along three different but not independent causal pathways . . . each causal sequence is *likely* to occur at different temporal points in the relationship" (pp. 250–251, italics in original). The following listings are summaries of points in his theory:

1. Beginning date rape
   a. Occurs in the first few dates at the beginning of a relationship.
   b. Given that most college students do not expect to have sexual intercourse during the first date, when rape does occur, the male may have dated the woman with the intention of raping her, realizing that such an action is less likely to be labeled as rape than would the action of a stranger-rapist.
   c. Beginning date rapists may also have a need for more, and for more varied, sexual experiences (Kanin, 1967).
   d. Women who date or have sex with a large number of different males increase their chances of exposure to a sexually aggressive male who commits a beginning date rape.
2. Early date rape
   a. Occurs early in the relationship.
   b. Couple is still establishing the rules of their relationship.
   c. Males view the world in a more sexualized manner than do females; hence a man may perceive sexual intent when the woman felt she communicated none.
   d. Such males want more sexual contact, and they assume that their dates have similar desires but disguise them and feign disinterest.
   e. If misconceptions were all that were involved, however, and the woman made it clear that she was misunderstood, most males would probably cease and desist. But men who engage in date rape at this stage may be poorer in coping with sexual frustration and impulse control. Foreplay has led to sexual arousal, which is mixed with emotions of surprise,

anger, and embarrassment over being denied consensual sexual intercourse. Under these circumstances, the sexually aggressive male may have reduced impulse control. Their belief systems encourage them to take what they want. They rape.

f. Women who are socially anxious may be more vulnerable to early rape, because they are hesitant to signal their displeasure early enough to inhibit the man from rape. Expressions of pain and pleading may only heighten the man's sexual arousal.

3. Relational date rape
   a. Couple has been dating for some time.
   b. They believe they know what to expect from each other.
   c. The motivation to date this woman by this man was not solely to have sexual intercourse with her.
   d. Exchange and social comparison processes are likely the causal factors. Some males who have been exclusively dating and showing affection toward a woman for a period of time may begin to feel shortchanged if intercourse does not occur.
   e. Most people who have been dating for a long period of time expect their relationship to develop toward marriage. One sign of movement, at least for the male, is sexual intercourse. In fact, for both genders, relationships in which sex did not occur are judged to be less serious (Peplau, Rubin, & Hill, 1977).
   f. If consensual sexual intercourse does not occur over the long term, the male may feel the situation is inequitable but may be unwilling to end the relationship because of his investment of time, energy, or resources.
   g. Social comparison processes may contribute, also. The male assumes that other men in similar relationships are sexually involved with their partners. The male may even compare himself with the woman's prior partners.
   h. Because of a desire to give the relationship momentum, sometime during the couple's usual "petting," the male will force sexual intercourse.
   i. The woman who abstains in a long-term relationship is likely to have conservative sexual values. But she may waver and give mixed messages.

comprehensive and representative studies to date (Koss et al., 1988) administered the Sexual Experiences Survey (Koss & Oros, 1982) to a national sample of more than 3,000 women. Of these women, 15% or around 200 reported having been raped as adults at least one time in their life. An impressive portion of these victims—85%—knew their assailant.

Some women may not label the assault a rape because they blame themselves for contributing to its occurrence—either through being naive or having placed themselves, through excessive drinking, for example, in an unsafe situation. A woman from Nevada told a *New York Times* reporter (Gross, 1991) that she did not call what happened to her "rape" until many years later. In contemplating what happened she:

1. Figured she had made a stupid mistake by agreeing to drive a fellow college student home from a party.
2. Wondered if she had led him on by going into his house.
3. Asked herself if she could have fought back more vigorously when he threw her on the bed and forced her to have sexual intercourse.
4. Felt embarrassed rather than angry after the attack was over, and apologized for "not wanting sex."

Date rape: a special case

We may think of "date rape" as a specific type of acquaintance rape, in the sense that a more defined relationship exists between the two parties than in the case of two routine acquaintances (Bechhofer & Parrot, 1991). And even though the mass media have recently alerted the public to the fact that date rape does exist, misunderstandings about it still prevail.

Contrary to popular opinion, date rape does not just occur on first dates. C.A. Skelton (1982) found that 36% occurred on a first date or by an acquaintance, 26% by an occasional date, and 31% by a regular suitor. Thus, any level of familiarity is possible—the couple may be on a blind date, or they may be intimate partners involved in a long-term relationship. Mary Koss and her colleagues reported in 1988 that of those victims of acquaintance rape, 35% were attacked by men they had been dating steadily. Another 29% of the sample were raped by men they knew such as a co-worker, a neighbor, or a friend with whom they were not romantically involved. One fourth of the victims had dated their assailant casually, and 11% were violated by either their husband or a family member. Note that of these victims—all of them victims of acquaintance rape—almost 70% were raped by men with whom they were romantically involved, or at least were dating. Another study (Muehlenhard, 1987) discovered that those dates that led to sexual aggression usually occurred in couples who had known each other almost a year.

Acquaintance rape and date rape are not rare occurrences. Do they possess qualities other than the relationship that distinguish them from rapes by strangers?

Unique qualities of the acquaintance rape

Only recently have researchers begun to examine in detail exactly what acquaintance rape is like. Some researchers have further identified important differences in the causes of date rape as a function of the type of dating relationship (see Box 2). When compared with rapes committed by strangers, a few important differences emerge. These include characteristics of the rape itself, reactions of the rape victim, and the perceptions of outside observers regarding the rape.

Compared to rapes by strangers, acquaintance rapes possess several unique characteristics. For example, the type of coercion displayed by the rapist is usually different. Although rapes by strangers more often employ verbal threats, physical violence, and weapons, rapes by acquaintances usually reflect more subtle types of coercion (Muehlenhard & Schrag, 1991) (see Box 3).

Box 3: The Profile of the Date Rape

Which seems more likely?

The victimizer:

1. is more sexually active than other males.
2. treats a woman as if she's his property, and gets angry when another man pays attention to her.
3. has a history of antisocial behavior; displays a lot of anger toward women.
4. subscribes to rape myths' acceptance of violence and similar attitudes, such as "Real men don't listen to 'no.'"
5. misperceives the actions of others, interprets passivity as permission.
6. denies that he has engaged in rape (in one study, cited by D. Goleman, 1989, only 17 of 1,152 male college students admitted to using physical force to have sexual intercourse when the woman didn't want to).
7. may have been drinking heavily (Norris, 1989); "The degree of intoxication of the man is the single most important factor in determining whether acquaintance rape will occur" (Bechhofer & Parrot, 1991, p. 23).

The victim:

1. is in a new environment, without friends.
2. may lack self-esteem (Skelton, 1982) or have poor social adjustment (Rogers, 1984).
3. is not good at asserting herself; does not communicate limits of acceptable behavior; may give mixed messages; does not fight back (Charlene Muehlenhard found in her study that the most powerful tactic is the statement: "This is rape and I'm calling the cops."").
4. may be drunk, fostering an assumption that further sexual activity is consensual (Norris, 1989).

Koss et al. (1988) found that the most common type of strategy used by the latter type of rapists was holding the victim down or twisting her arm. Although about one third of acquaintance rapes do, indeed, involve verbal abuse, according to Koss's survey, this percentage is perceptibly lower than the 54% of rapes by strangers that include verbal threats. Many times the kind of verbal threats used in acquaintance rapes and date rapes are different from those by strangers; they more likely capitalize on verbal "manipulation." For example, one investigation (Mosher & Anderson, 1986) discovered that 44% of the date rapists in their sample admitted telling the woman that a refusal to have sex with him would change the way he felt about her; 34% of the men in this sample threatened to end the relationship. It seems that another common strategy used by date rapists is to "just do it," even after the woman protests, essentially ignoring her pleas (Muehlenhard, 1987; Rapaport & Burkhart, 1984).

A rape is a rape and its consequences cannot be trivialized just because of some prior expectations by the woman or prior relationship with the assailant.

Acquaintance rapes often occur at different times from rapes by strangers. Date rapes, in particular, are more likely to occur on weekends, between the hours of 10 p.m. and 1 a.m. They are also more likely to occur at isolated locations, in a car, or at the home of the assailant (Harney & Muehlenhard, 1991). They may last much longer—sometimes 4 hours or more (Seligmann, 1984). These factors may contribute to another difference found between rapes by acquaintances and those by strangers— the number of offenses. Although date rapes and acquaintance rapes usually involve only one perpetrator, the rapist is more likely to commit a number of rapes over a period of time (Koss, 1988b). But the incidence of "party rape"—the gang rape of a woman by several acquaintances—has only recently been recognized as prevalent, at colleges as well as elsewhere. J.K. Ehrhart and B.R. Sandler (1985) describe the cruel rape of a young college woman:

> It was her first fraternity party. The beer flowed freely and she had much more to drink than she had planned. It was hot and crowded and the party spread out all over the house, so that when three men asked her to go upstairs, she went with them. They took her into the bedroom, locked the door and began to undress her. Groggy with alcohol, her feeble protests were ignored as the three men raped her. When they finished, they put her in the hallway, naked, locking her clothes in the bedroom. (1985, p. 2)

In studying such incidents, Ehrhart and Sandler's interviewers were told by some campus officials that "it happens almost every week." Peggy R. Sanday (1990) reports that this type of gang rape is often referred to as "training" and is part of the campus party culture. Because many—if not most—of the victims end up dropping out of college shortly after being victimized and few such gang rapes are ever officially reported, the inclusion of these rapes is likely to be missed in most surveys.

Reactions of the rape victim

Victims of rapes by dates or acquaintances report high levels of anger and depression, just as victims of rapes by strangers do (Koss, 1988b). But partly as a result of experiencing less violence from the rapist, they also report they weren't quite as scared as were recipients of attacks by strangers. It seems fruitless to us to speculate as to which is worse. As B. Katz (1991) notes, the survivor of a stranger rape may have an easier time seeing her own victimization as a more random and less personal event. In contrast, the date-rape victim may have her identity as a social being brought into question—is she competent to function in relationships?

Interestingly, victims of date rapes did not differ from those of rapes by strangers with respect to their use of so-called passive forms of resistance (for example, using reasoning or pleading, crying or sobbing, or turning cold toward the other). Koss discovered that a large percentage of all victims reported resorting to such behaviors. Another common strategy used by both types of victims involved physically struggling to get away. Although the victims of stranger rapes were more likely to use the more active types of resistance such as screaming or trying to run away, neither type of victim used active resistance procedures very often. This is unfortunate [because] these active forms of resistance may be the most effective ways to avoid a rape (Bart & O'Brien, 1984; Levine-MacCombie & Koss, 1986).

Of course, one reason why victims of acquaintance rapes may be less inclined to resist actively is a direct function of the characteristics of the rape. Before a rape can be resisted, the danger must be identified. Many women find sharing their company with a male on a Friday or Saturday night a common occurrence, in fact nothing out of the ordinary. If the situation is not perceived to be dangerous at first, the act of resistance is altered. Initial reactions to intrusions on one's limits may be that such intrusions are harmless (Rozée, Bateman & Gilmore, 1991). Unfortunately, victims who wait too long before protesting are viewed as both desiring sex and sharing the blame for the rape (Shotland & Goodstein, 1983).

More recent estimates suggest that in most rapes the victim and her assailant were familiar to each other.

As implied earlier, the impact of the rape upon the victim's life is somewhat different when the rapist is an acquaintance rather than a stranger. Victims of the latter type of rapes are more likely to seek support from others to help them deal with the experience. Although three fourths of the women raped by someone totally unknown to them later discussed the experience with some other person, only about one half of those raped by an acquaintance did so (Koss, 1988b). This difference is important, because talking about the ordeal may be the single most important therapeutic behavior that a victim can do afterward (Davis & Friedman, 1985; Koss, 1988b). And although victims of rapes by strangers are more likely to seek professional help from a rape crisis center or the police, neither of the two types of victims are likely to do so very often. In Koss's study, of all the victims willing to talk about their experiences, approximately one fourth of the victims of stranger rape sought this type of help, but only 3% of victims involved with acquaintance rape sought such help, even though 62% of the stranger rape victims and 38% of the acquaintance rape victims felt they should obtain some type of therapy to help them deal with their trauma.

Once more, in these differences, we see the possibility that victims of acquaintance rape, by remaining silent, are reflecting heightened feelings of guilt and self-blame (Jenkins & Dambrot, 1987). Even though their physical suffering may be less, the psychological costs may be greater than those of stranger rape victims, whose open discussion of their experience alleviates some of the psychological symptoms.

General reactions to the date rape

"You can't be raped by someone you know." This is a common belief, but many women can testify to its inaccuracy. Most were shocked that their "friend" could do such a thing. Not only may such rape victims begin to question seriously their ability to judge others, but people aware of the rape may also generate doubts of their own. Unfortunately, many of the characteristics of the interaction contribute to some observers even justifying the rape by diminishing the blame to the rapist. For example, in one survey of high-school students, 43% of males and 32% of females believe that it is acceptable for a man to force a woman to have sex if they have dated for a long time (Giarrusso, Johnson, Goodchilds & Zellman, 1979). More than half the males in the above survey also believed rape to be at least somewhat justifiable if the woman was "leading the man on." Other aspects that may lead some individuals to justify a sexual assault are the use of alcohol by either the man or the woman and the man's spending a lot of money on the woman. Given these circumstances, some people are willing to dismiss the sexual interaction as something less than a rape. . . .

Blaming the victim . . . is a robust phenomenon. Especially when the two people are a dating couple, people often believe that the woman—somehow, some way—should have known the man's intentions. Women and men may differ in their reactions to different types of rape, as reflected in a study by P.A. Tetreault and M.A. Barnett (1987). In this study, undergraduate students were given scenarios depicting a sexual encounter. Half of the subjects received a description of an acquaintance rape, while the other half read about a woman victimized by a total stranger. After all of the students had read the scenario, they watched the same videotape of a rape victim (actually portrayed by an actress) in order to add authenticity to the study. Finally, they were asked to give their opinions about the encounter.

Acquaintance rape and date rape are not rare occurrences.

Results of the study were quite intriguing. Females who were exposed to the stranger rape were more likely to believe that the situation they had read about was more serious, and was, indeed, rape more than females who were exposed to the acquaintance rape. Females viewing the acquaintance rape also reported blaming the victim more and liking her less. Males, on the other hand, reacted in just the opposite way. They felt like the acquaintance rape was the more serious crime, and definitely rape. They tended to blame the victim of the stranger rape more, and to like her less. The men's attributions were apparently influenced by a greater devaluation of the stranger rape victim (Calhoun & Townsley, 1991). In another study that examined differing levels of men's sexual arousal to depictions of rape, it was found that men show just as much arousal to depictions of acquaintance rape as they do to portrayals of consenting sex (Check & Malamuth, 1983). It seems clear that two very different processes are working here. How can such results be explained? J.V.P. Check and N.M. Malamuth (1983) cite societal standards as the culprit. . . . Because standards for how men and women should act are different, responses to such personal violations may be very different. Women are taught that they are supposed to be caring and sensitive without becoming too "available." They are also taught to expect the man to test the boundaries of their "availability." Women confronted with other women who have been raped by an acquaintance, therefore, may view her as somehow breaking the rules. Men, on the other hand, may believe that it's all right for a woman to be sexually involved—as long as she is in a legitimate relationship. Inevitably, having sexual relations with a stranger (presumably no matter the conditions) is breaking the rules to men. Either way, everyone loses.

Even though their physical suffering may be less, the psychological costs [for acquaintance rape victims] may be greater than those of stranger rape victims.

In several other investigations that looked at differences between men and women in how they view a rape between acquaintances (Jenkins & Dambrot, 1987; Weir, 1991), sex differences were found. It seems that, in general, men are less likely to perceive a situation in which a man forces his date to have sex as rape and are more likely to perceive that the woman desired sexual intercourse. Perhaps date rape is more serious, therefore, because they believe the woman is acting in a way that may be harmful to the man.

Whose fault is it?

Especially in Western society, people may become consumed with the idea that everything happens for a reason, that there has to be an answer to the question "Why?" When one is raped by an acquaintance or date, attributing blame to someone seems unavoidable, both by those involved and by outside observers.

Unfortunately, the someone who is blamed is often the victim. A writer for *Time* magazine, John Leo (1987), illustrates the subtle bias against the victim. He states that, "Like many victims, Susan was unwary and alone too soon with a man she barely knew" (p. 77). Was Susan in a car on a deserted highway? No. She was 19 years old, in summer school at a college where she met a man in the dorm cafeteria and went to his dorm room that evening to watch the news on TV and get acquainted.

Even the esteemed Ann Landers, at least back in 1985, expressed a conventional "woman at risk" view when she wrote in response: "And now, at the risk of sounding hilariously square, I'd like to suggest that the woman who 'repairs to some private place for a few drinks and a little shared affection' had, by her acceptance of such a cozy invitation, given the man reason to believe she is a candidate for whatever he might have in mind" (1985, p. 5).

Rather than communicating a message that women shouldn't take risks, society should examine the standards it uses in courtship and dating. These provide some explanations for the emergence of date rape.

References

Bart, P.B., & O'Brien, P.H. (1984). Stopping rape: Effective avoidance strategies. *Signs: Journal of Women in Culture and Society, 10,* 83–101.

Bechhofer, L., & Parrot, A. (1991). What is acquaintance rape? In A. Parrot & L. Bechhofer (Eds.), *Acquaintance rape: The hidden crime* (pp. 9–25). New York: John Wiley.

Calhoun, K.S., & Townsley, R.M. (1991). Attributions of responsibility for acquaintance rape. In A. Parrot & L. Bechhofer (Eds.), *Acquaintance rape: The hidden crime* (pp. 57–69). New York: John Wiley.

Check, J.V.P., & Malamuth, N.M. (1983). Sex role stereotyping and reactions to depictions of stranger versus acquaintance rape. *Journal of Personality and Social Psychology, 45,* 344–356.

Davis, R.C., & Friedman, L.N. (1985). The emotional aftermath of crime and violence. In C.R. Figley (Ed.), *Trauma and its wake: The study and treatment of post-traumatic stress disorder* (pp. 90–111). New York: Brunner/Mazel.

Ehrhart, J.K., & Sandler, B.R. (1985). *Campus gang rape: Party games?* Washington, DC: Association of American Colleges.

Giarrusso, R., Johnson, P.B., Goodchilds, J.D., & Zellman, G. (1979, April). *Adolescent cues and signals: Sex and assault.* Paper presented at the meetings of the Western Psychological Association, San Diego.

Goleman, D. (1989, August 29). When the rapist is not a stranger. *The New York Times,* pp. 13, 21.

Goodman, E. (1987, September 29). Jessica Hahn story has ring of truth. *Lawrence Journal-World,* p. 5A.

Gross, J. (1991, May 28). Even the victim can be slow to recognize rape. *The New York Times,* p. A8.

Harney, P.A., & Muehlenhard, C.L. (1991). Factors that increase the likelihood of victimization. In A. Parrot & L. Bechhofer (Eds.), *Acquaintance rape: The hidden crime* (pp. 159–175). New York: John Wiley.

Jenkins, M.J., & Dambrot, F.H. (1987). The attribution of date rape: Observer's attitudes and sexual experiences and the dating situation. *Journal of Applied Social Psychology, 17,* 875–895.

Kanin, E.J. (1967). Reference groups and sex conduct norm violations. *Sociological Quarterly, 8,* 495–504.

Katz, B.L. (1991). The psychological impact of stranger versus nonstranger rape on victims' recovery. In A. Parrot & L. Bechhofer (Eds.), *Acquaintance rape: The hidden crime* (pp. 251–269). New York: John Wiley.

Koss, M.P. (1985). The hidden rape victim: Personality, attitudinal, and situational characteristics. *Psychology of Women Quarterly, 9,* 193–212.

Koss, M.P. (1988a, August). *Criminal victimization among women. Impact on health status and medical services usage.* Paper presented at the annual meeting of the American Psychological Association, Atlanta, GA.

Koss, M.P. (1988b). Hidden rape: Incidence, prevalence, and descriptive characteristics of sexual aggression and victimization in a national sample of college students. In A.W. Burgess (Ed.), *Sexual assault* (Vol. II, pp. 3–25). New York: Garland.

Koss, M.P., Dinero, T.E., Seibel, C.A., & Cox, S. (1988). Stranger and acquaintance rape: Are there differences in the victim's experience? *Psychology of Women Quarterly, 12,* 1–24.

Koss, M.P., & Oros, C. (1982). Sexual Experiences Survey: A research instrument investigating aggression and victimization. *Journal of Consulting and Clinical Psychology, 50,* 445–457.

Landers, A. (1985, July 29). Date rape issues: Another view. *Lawrence Journal-World,* p. 5.

Landers, A. (1987, October 8). "Horsing around" was prelude to date rape. *Kansas City Times,* p. B-8.

Landers, A. (1988, April 24). Woman shares insight on dating married men. *Lawrence Journal-World,* p. 5A.

Leo, J. (1987, March 23). When the date turns into rape. *Time,* p. 77.

Levine-MacCombie, J., & Koss, M.P. (1986). Acquaintance rape: Effective avoidance strategies. *Psychology of Women Quarterly, 10,* 311–320.

Lewin, T. (1991, May 27). Tougher laws mean more cases are called rape. *The New York Times,* p. 9.

Mosher, D.L., & Anderson, R.D. (1986). Macho personality, sexual aggression, and reactions to guided imagery of realistic rape. *Journal of Research in Personality, 20,* 77–94.

Muehlenhard, C.L. (1987, October). Date rape: The familiar perpetrator. In *Our sexuality newsletter,* supplement to R. Crooks & K. Baur, *Our sexuality* (3rd ed.). Menlo Park, CA: Benjamin/Cummings.

Muehlenhard, C.L. (1988). Misinterpreted dating behaviors and the risk of date rape. *Journal of Social and Clinical Psychology, 6,* 20–37.

Muehlenhard, C.L., & Cook, S.W. (1988). Men's self-reports of unwanted sexual activity. *Journal of Sex Research, 24,* 58–72.

Muehlenhard, C.L., & Schrag, J.L. (1991). Nonviolent sexual coercion. In A. Parrot & L. Bechhofer (Eds.), *Acquaintance rape: The hidden crime* (pp. 115–128). New York: John Wiley.

Norris, J. (1989, August). *Acquaintance rape: Effects of victim's and assailant's alcohol consumption.* Paper presented at the meetings of the American Psychological Association, New Orleans.

Peplau, L.A., Rubin, Z., & Hill, C.T. (1977). Sexual intimacy in dating relationships. *Journal of Social Issues, 33*(2), 86–109.

Rapaport, K., & Burkhart, B.R. (1984). Personality and attitudinal characteristics of sexually coercive college males. *Journal of Abnormal Psychology, 93,* 216–221.

Richardson, D., & Campbell, J.L. (1982). Alcohol and rape: The effect of alcohol on attributions of blame for rape. *Personality and Social Psychology Bulletin, 8,* 468–476.

Rogers, L.C. (1984). *Sexual victimization: Social and psychological effects in college women.* Unpublished doctoral dissertation, Auburn University.

Rozée P.D., Bateman, P., & Gilmore, T. (1991). The personal perspective of acquaintance rape prevention: A three-tier approach. In A. Parrot & L. Bechhofer (Eds.), *Acquaintance rape: The hidden crime* (pp. 337–354). New York: John Wiley.

Sanday, P.R. (1990). *Fraternity gang rape: Sex, brotherhood, and privilege on campus.* New York: New York University Press.

Seligmann, J. (1984, April 9). The date who rapes. *Newsweek,* pp. 91–92.

Shotland, R.L. (1989). A model of the causes of date rape in developing and close relationships. In C. Hendrick (Ed.), *Close relationships* (pp. 247–270). Newbury Park, CA: Sage.

Shotland R.L., & Goodstein, L. (1983). Just because she doesn't want to doesn't mean it's rape: An experimentally-based causal model of perception of rape in a dating situation. *Social Psychology Quarterly, 46,* 220–232.

Skelton, C.A. (1982). *Situational and personological correlates of sexual victimization in college women.* Unpublished doctoral dissertation, Auburn University.

Tetreault, P.A., & Barnett, M.A. (1987). Reactions to stranger and acquaintance rape. *Psychology of Women Quarterly, 11,* 353–358.

Weir, J.A. (1991). *The effects of focus of attention, legal procedures, and individual differences on judgments in a rape case.* Unpublished doctoral dissertation, University of Kansas.

2

Claims of Date Rape Can Trivialize the Problem of Sexual Violence

David R. Carlin

David R. Carlin is a columnist for Commonweal, *a biweekly Catholic periodical.*

Rape has been traditionally defined as forced, nonconsensual sex. However, many academic researchers have claimed that acquaintance rape and date rape can result from verbal and emotional pressure on the part of the assailant. Defining date rape as a possible outcome of emotional manipulation implies that rape can occur even when consent is given. Failure to recognize the difference between a man who uses verbal persuasion and a man who uses physical force or weapons to demand sex can trivialize the problem of sexual violence.

Like many others, I have been puzzled by the theory and practice of date rape. When I first heard mention of date rape a few years back, I was a bit surprised that such a phenomenon had become a major problem. But my surprise quickly wore off as I reflected that this was the sort of thing that was bound to happen, given society's widespread moral subjectivism and consequently permissive sexual code.

But then I was surprised again when I read about astonishingly high rates of date rape on college campuses. In some places 25 to 50 percent of all undergraduate females had been victims of date rape. Now I was willing to believe (in fact I was eager to believe) that young men in college were not as gentlemanly as they were back in the days when I was alive. Yet I found it hard to believe they had become quite that bad.

A new definition of rape

My credulity was strained even more when I read the explanations for these high numbers given by critics of date rape research. According to

From David R. Carlin, "Date Rape Fallacies: Can There Be Purely Voluntary Acts?" *Commonweal*, February 25, 1994. Reprinted with permission of *Commonweal*.

the critics, these astonishing figures are a function not of a new kind of behavior among college men but of a new definition of rape among researchers. While "rape" used to mean coerced, nonconsensual sex, it now also includes having sex when you'd really rather not but you've been talked into it by a partner who has utilized any of a large number of items in the seducer's classical bag of tricks, e.g., flattery, promises, arguments, appeals to pity, reminders of past promises, threats to break off the relationship, etc. In other words, rape occurs even when consent is given, provided this consent is influenced by external pressure and is not simply the result of internal desire.

I found it difficult to believe that academic researchers could be as intellectually dishonest as the critics alleged. I suspected these critics were antifeminist right-wingers who were making it all up.

But of course it really isn't a matter of dishonesty; rather it's a matter of redefinition. The date-rape theorists are saying: "Hitherto the world has had an inadequate conception of rape, for that conception has not taken into consideration the full range of diminished consent that can be involved in a sexual act. Nor has it recognized that these lesser forms of involuntariness differ in degree only, not in kind, from the more extreme form involved in the classical conception of rape."

The theorists then note that the classical definition of rape was created by men, that is, by people who are inevitably insensitive to the many varieties of sexual involuntariness that may be experienced by women. By contrast, the new expanded and improved definition is created by women. The old definition defined the crime from the point of view of the perpetrator, the new from the point of view of the victim.

There still remains a world of difference between a smooth talker on the one hand and a man holding a knife to your throat on the other.

When I had got this far in my reflections I had a moment of illumination. I saw the point, and I thought the point was valid—even though I continue to be troubled by the use of the word "rape" to cover the whole range of events. For no matter how true the new feminist analysis might be, there still remains a world of difference between a smooth talker on the one hand and a man holding a knife to your throat on the other. Calling them both rapists may be a fine way of highlighting the malignity of the former, but it is also a way of trivializing the criminality of the latter. Nonetheless, I am willing to grant that the date-rape theorists have made an important discovery.

But once we start noting degrees of involuntariness, where do we stop? When is consent to a sexual act fully voluntary? For that matter, when is consent to any act fully voluntary? How many moments per day do you do purely and simply what you want to do—not what your spouse would like you to do, or your children, or your boss, or your co-workers, or the police officer, or the state legislature? Not many moments, I'd guess. Of course when we comply with the wishes of these others, we are often complying more or less with our own wishes. Our actions in these cases have a double source: internal inclination plus external pressure. But we need both; for when the latter is absent, the former is usually not strong enough to compel us to action. I won't say there is no such thing as a purely 100-percent voluntary action, just as I won't say there is no such thing as a purely 100-percent altruistic action. If such deeds exist, they are the rarest things in the world. Yet to recognize that altruism is almost always alloyed with egoism is not to deny that there are altruistic acts and persons; nor is it to deny that there are fundamental differences between Mother Teresa and Stalin. Similarly, to recognize that voluntariness is almost always mixed with elements of involuntariness is not to deny that there is a real and extremely important distinction between voluntary and involuntary actions. Meeting one's contractual obligations may contain elements of the involuntary, but it is still radically different from being a slave or a prisoner.

The question of free choice

The ideal of the purely voluntary sex act is part and parcel of the contemporary liberal belief that actions are morally sound only when they arise from the free choice of autonomous individuals. According to this view, if I allow others to impose their values or preferences upon me, I am not truly autonomous; my choices are not really my choices; hence my actions are morally defective.

But this quest for autonomy is a will o' the wisp, for human beings are essentially incapable of being purely autonomous. Humans are social beings all the way down; and to be a member of society is to be part of a system of mutual controls; hence it is to be something less than fully autonomous. At bottom, then, the desire for autonomy is the desire to live outside of society. As Aristotle said a long time ago, the one who lives outside society is either below human nature or above it, either a beast or a god.

So let's have one-and-a-half rousing cheers for the feminists exploring the many degrees of involuntariness involved in sex. But to the degree they get their effort mixed up with the impossible ideal of perfect autonomy and pure voluntariness, they are in grave danger of giving their important work the aspect of absurdity.

3

Acquaintance Rape Has Been Increasing

Emilie Buchwald, Pamela R. Fletcher, and Martha Roth

Emilie Buchwald, Pamela R. Fletcher, and Martha Roth are the editors of Transforming a Rape Culture, *from which this viewpoint is excerpted.*

Several recent studies on sexual assault reveal an upsurge in rape in the United States. The number of reported rapes has increased by at least 88 percent since the early 1970s, and between one hundred thousand and six hundred thousand rapes occur annually. Moreover, a majority of these rapes—between 70 and 80 percent—are committed by intimates or acquaintances of the victim. Until American society seriously addresses the causes of sexual violence, rape will remain pervasive.

Not a day goes by without a story in the media about sexual violence against women and children. Do rape and sexual assault truly permeate this society, or are we hearing about the sensationalized, isolated cases? Has the rate of sexual violence really increased? Current statistics about the incidence of sexual violence include two programs administered by the U.S. Department of Justice—the Uniform Crime Report and the National Crime Victimization Survey—and other recent studies focused on rape and child sexual abuse. What do these studies and the analyses of their numbers tell us?

The Uniform Crime Report (UCR)[1] The FBI's Uniform Crime Report data is compiled from over 16,000 law enforcement agencies covering 96 percent of the nation's population. Baseless or unfounded complaints are excluded from crime counts. A frequent, recurring criticism of the UCR figures has been that rape is notoriously underreported to the police; thus, the UCR figures represent only a portion of the actual number of rape victimizations.[2]

• In 1991, the UCR recorded 106,593 rapes. *That's 292 rapes each day of the year, or 12 rapes every hour, or 1 rape every 5 minutes.*

• The UCR reported *1.5 million female survivors* of forcible rape or forcible rape attempts in this country, during the twenty-year period of

1972 to 1991 alone. These are the most conservative numbers available and should be considered *the baseline or minimum* rape figure.

• The number of rapes reported to the UCR has risen steadily over most of the past twenty years: From 1972 to 1991, there was a *128 percent increase* in the number of reported rapes. During the same time period, the forcible rape rate per 100,000 inhabitants increased 88 percent.

The *National Crime Victimization Surrey (NCVS)*[3], the largest nationally representative, household-interview crime survey in the United States, is administered by the Bureau of the Census for the Bureau of Justice Statistics.

• The NCVS reported 171,420 rapes for 1991. *That's 469 rapes each day of the year, or 19 each hour, or 1 rape every 3.5 minutes.*

• The NCVS recorded *2.3 million rapes* of females during the years from 1973 to 1987. Thus, in a fifteen-year period, the NCVS recorded almost 1 million more cases of rape than the twenty-year UCR numbers. For a comparable twenty-year period, the number of female rape survivors in this country would be *3 million women for that twenty-year period alone.*

• Intimates (husbands, ex-spouses, boyfriends, ex-boyfriends) committed 20 percent of rapes, acquaintances 50 percent, and strangers 30 percent of the rapes reported to NCVS between 1987–1991.[4]

The NWS [National Women's Study] found that only 22 percent of rape victims were assaulted by someone they had never seen before or did not know well.

Rape in America: A Report to the Nation[5] The National Women's Study (NWS), issued in 1992, was conducted by the Crime Victims Research and Treatment Center. The respondents were women 18 years and older at the time of the initial survey.

• Thirteen percent of women surveyed reported having been victims of at least one completed rape. Thirty-nine percent of this group had been raped more than once. The majority of rape cases occurred during childhood and adolescence, with 29 percent of all forcible rapes occurring when the victim was less than eleven years old, and another 32 percent of rapes occurring between 11 and 17 years of age.

• The NWS found that *only 22 percent of rape victims were assaulted by someone they had never seen before or did not know well.* Nine percent were raped by husbands or ex-husbands, 11 percent by their fathers or stepfathers, 10 percent by boyfriends or ex-boyfriends, 16 percent by other relatives, and 29 percent by other non-relatives, such as friends and neighbors.

• Only 16 percent, or approximately one out of about six rapes, were ever reported to police. If the Uniform Crime Report numbers represent only one of about six rapes actually committed, the true number of rapes in the United States each year is likely to be in the range of 639,500. *At that rate over a twenty-year period, there would be more than 12 million American women rape survivors.*

Other facts about sexual abuse and rape prosecution and conviction

• The National Committee for Prevention of Child Abuse in its 1991 survey of child protective service agencies listed 404,100 reports of child sexual abuse. These reports *do not take into account* sexual abuse by non-caretakers.[6]

• About 16,000 women a year have abortions as a result of rape or incest.[7]

• One in 100 rapists is sentenced to more than one year in prison.[8]

• Almost one quarter of *convicted rapists* are not sentenced to prison but instead are released on probation.[8]

Are we really living in a rape culture? Rape is a pervasive fact of American life, and its incidence is growing dramatically. The most conservative figures show an 88 percent increase in the rate of forcible rape per 100,000 inhabitants over the past twenty years. There are, at minimum, 105,000 rapes annually in the United States and perhaps more than 630,000. In the time it took to read these statistics at least one person has been raped. Over a twenty-year period, as many as 12 million women and children—nearly 10 percent of the current female population of the United States—have been raped. Both the victims and their attackers carry the fact of rape through their lives and, one can argue, through their families' lives as well. We will continue to live in a rape culture until our society understands and chooses to eradicate the sources of sexual violence in this culture.

Notes

1. Federal Bureau of Investigation, United States Department of Justice, *Crime in the United States, 1991,* August 30, 1992, pp. 14, 17, 24, 58, Table 1.—Index of Crimes, United States, 1972–1991.

2. Larry Baron and Murray A. Straus, *Four Theories of Rape in American Society* (New Haven: Yale University Press, 1989), p. 27.

3. A National Crime Victimization Survey Report, *Criminal Victimization in the United States, 1991,* December 1992, NCJ-139563, pp. 72–75, 79, 148–149; United States Department of Justice, Bureau of Justice Statistics, *Female Victims of Violent Crime,* by Caroline Wolf Harlow, January 1991, NCJ-126826, pp. 1–3, 7.

4. Ronet Bachman, "Female Victims of Violence," paper presented at the 1993 Annual Meeting of the American Society of Criminology, November 1993, p. 23, Table 11.

5. National Victim Center and the Crime Victims Research and Treatment Center, *Rape in America: A Report to the Nation,* April 23, 1992, pp. 1–16. A complete Methodology Overview is given on page 15.

6. The National Resource Center on Child Sexual Abuse, brochure, 107 Lincoln Street, Huntsville, Alabama 35801, 1-800-KIDS-006.

7. "Facts in Brief: Abortion in the United States," The Alan Guttmacher Institute, 1993, p. 1.

8. Report of the Majority Staff of the Senate Judiciary Committee, "The Response to Rape: Detours on the Road to Equal Justice," May 1993, pp. 11, 25–60.

4

Rape Is Too Broadly Defined

Wendy McElroy

Wendy McElroy is a contributing editor to the libertarian magazine Liberty, *and author of the books* Freedom, Feminism and the State *and* XXX: A Woman's Right to Pornography.

During the 1960s, feminism rightly challenged the assumption that rape only happens to "bad" women who walk alone after dark and then are sexually assaulted by violent strangers. However, by the 1980s, radical feminists had redefined rape as a tool that men use to subjugate women, arguing that America is essentially a "rape culture." Moreover, rape came to be defined as sexual contact that could involve verbal persuasion or harassment with no physical coercion. Such a redefinition blurs the distinction between rape and seduction and fosters hostility between men and women. Rape must be understood as nonconsensual sex resulting from physical force or threat of injury.

R ape is an abomination that no civilized society can tolerate. In the '60s, feminists broke down the old, puritanical mythology of rape. They shattered the presumption that only bad girls who walked alone at night got raped, and exploded the notion that all rapists were seedy men who lurked in alleys. In fact, *every* woman, from infancy to the grave, is vulnerable to attack, even in her own home. And rapists can be hard-working husbands or apple-cheeked boys next door, not just hardened criminals and psychopaths. Indeed, the victim usually knows her assailant.

In the place of the old mythology of rape, '60s feminism offered facts and practical help for women in pain. Their hotlines and crisis centers did something neither the legal system nor new research could: they talked to raped women, and let them know they were not alone.

As a woman who has been raped, I owe a debt to '60s feminism. I emerged from the experience in one piece largely because of the groundwork feminists had already created for rape victims. I learned that I had a right to be angry, not only at the man who raped me, but also at the laws and cultural attitudes that sheltered him and not me. From feminism I learned an irreplaceable lesson: *What happened to me was not my fault.*

From Wendy McElroy, "The New Mythology of Rape," *Liberty*, September 1994. Reprinted with permission.

But in the past two decades, a disturbing change has taken place in feminism's approach to rape. Rape used to be considered a crime, a violation of normal life. Then, in the '70s, a theoretical groundwork was laid to place rape at the very heart of our culture. For the new feminists, rape was an expression of how the average man viewed the average woman. By the mid-'80s, rape had become thoroughly politicized: it was now viewed as a major weapon—perhaps *the* major weapon—by which the patriarchy keeps women in their place.

The New York Radical Feminists' manifesto exemplifies this change:

> It is no accident that the New York Radical Feminists, through the technique of consciousness-raising, discovered that rape is not a personal misfortune but an experience shared by all women in one form or another. When more than two people have suffered the same oppression the problem is no longer personal but political—and rape is a political matter. . . . [M]an is always uneasy and threatened by the possibility that woman will one day claim her full right to human existence, so he has found ways to enslave her. He has married her, and through the family, binds her to him as wife and mother to his children. He has kept her helpless and dependent, forcing her to work when he needed her labor, isolating her (physically and psychologically), and as a final proof of his power and her debasement as a possession, a thing, a chunk of meat, he has raped her. The act of rape is the logical expression of the essential relationship now existing between men and women. (Quoted in *Rape: The First Sourcebook for Feminists* by Mary Ann Manhart, p. 215)

Rape was no longer a crime committed by individuals against individuals. It had become part of class analysis.

Perhaps the most basic new myth about rape [is] that it is a crime with one cause: the general oppression of women by men.

In the conclusion to *Rape: The First Sourcebook for Feminists,* Mary Ann Manhart remarked on this shift:

> [T]he initial step in the feminist process is consciousness-raising and the final step is political action. . . . Consciousness-raising is a political act, and in turn, political action becomes consciousness-raising. . . . In a sense, rape is not a reformist but a revolutionary issue because our ultimate goal is to eliminate rape and that goal cannot be achieved without a revolutionary transformation of our society. It means a transformation of the family, the economic system, and the psychology of men and women so that sexual exploitation along with economic exploitation becomes impossible and even unimaginable. (p. 249–250)

In her near-legendary essay, "Rape: The All-American Crime," radical feminist Susan Griffin makes what no longer sounds like a radical or unusual claim:

> Indeed, the existence of rape in any form is beneficial to the ruling class of white males. For rape is a kind of terrorism which severely limits the freedom of women and makes women dependent on men. . . . This oppressive attitude towards women finds its institutionalization in the traditional family. *(Rape Victimology,* Leroy G. Schultz, ed., 1975, p. 3)

Rape had found its niche within a political ideology with a revolutionary agenda. No longer simply an abominable crime, it had become an accusation to be thrown wholesale at "white male culture" and all men.

By politicizing and collectivizing the pain of women, radical feminism is reversing the gains of the '60s, when the myths about rape and the barriers between men and women had a chance of being dissolved. Today, new myths and new barriers are being erected.

New myths for old

Any look at this new mythology should begin with Susan Brownmiller's seminal book of 1975, *Against Our Will,* which charts the history of rape from Neanderthal times to modern days, placing great emphasis on periods of war and crisis. *Against Our Will* is a watershed book, one which has been said to "give rape its history." Its radical thesis is that rape is the primary mechanism through which men—as a class—perpetuate their domination over women. According to Brownmiller, all men benefit from the fact that some men rape.

I understand how compelling this view of rape can be. At times, I've wanted to blame all men for the violence I experienced. Certainly, I was angry at all men.

But Brownmiller's theory of rape is wrong. And it is damaging to women.

Brownmiller makes three basic and interconnected claims:

- Rape is an arm of patriarchy;
- Men have created a "mass psychology" of rape; and
- Rape is a part of "normal" life.

I dispute each of these.

Is rape an arm of patriarchy? This is perhaps the most basic new myth about rape, that it is a crime with one cause: the general oppression of women by men. It is no longer politically correct to conduct studies on the causes of rape, because—as any right-thinking person knows—there is only one cause.

Decades ago, in the heyday of liberal feminism and sexual curiosity, the approach to research was more sophisticated. The Kinsey study of the 1950s classified seven types of rapists—assaultive, amoral, drunken, explosive, double-standard, mental-defective, and psychotic. And as recently as 1979, in *Men Who Rape: The Psychology of the Offender,* A. Nicholas Groth made a statement that sounds almost jarring to today's ears: "One of the most basic observations one can make regarding men who rape is that not all such offenders are alike" (p. 12).

Such studies are no longer in fashion. It is no longer proper to suggest that there can be as many motives for rape as there are for other violent crimes.

People murder for money, for love, out of jealousy or patriotism—the rationalizations come in all colors and shapes. Rape is every bit as complex. Men rape out of sexual hunger, from a need to prove themselves, from hatred of women, from a desire for revenge, as a political statement, from peer pressure. There is a constellation of possible motives for sexual assault, which become further blurred when you introduce drunkenness or other drug use to the equation.

Eldridge Cleaver defined his rape activity as "an insurrectionary act. It delighted me that I was defying and trampling upon the white man's law upon his system of values and that I was defiling his women. . . . I felt I was getting revenge" *(Soul on Ice,* 1965, p. 28). Contrast that with this comment in *The Crime and Consequences of Rape:*

> In acquaintance rapes, the brutality and violence . . . are usually absent. Since sex is the primary motivation in these cases, any classification of the motivation for rape would have to include sex in addition to power, anger, and sadism as motivating factors. (p. 44)

Feminism needs a theory that reconciles Cleaver's rapes with those of a drunken frat brother. We need a theory that explores the complexity of the issue, not one that oversimplifies it for the sake of a political agenda. Instead, radical feminists offer book after book of anecdotal, biased studies full of unproven blanket assertions that have acquired the status of truth through sheer repetition.

Armed with such ideological arrogance, radical feminists jettison all scientific method from their research. Susan Brownmiller asks, "Does one need scientific methodology in order to conclude that the anti-female propaganda that permeates our nation's cultural output promotes a climate in which acts of sexual hostility directed against women are not only tolerated but ideologically encouraged?" (p. 395). Her answer to the rhetorical question is plain.

We need a theory [about rape] that explores the complexity of the issue, not one that oversimplifies it for the sake of a political agenda.

And that answer is wrong. One needs scientific methodology to verify any empirical claim. Otherwise, all discussions devolve into opinion. Or worse, they become a barrier to real research conducted by people willing to reach conclusions based on data, not prejudice. Inconvenient issues like rape committed against men are also ignored, or sidestepped; all victims are considered, for political purposes, to be women. This is rather like the television interview in which Stokely Carmichael divided the world into the white oppressor and the black oppressed. When asked about the huge global population of Asians, he replied, "Consider them black."

Brownmiller's second myth is that men as a class have created a mass psychology of rape—that all men are rapists at heart, and all women their natural prey:

> Man's discovery that his genitalia could serve as a weapon to generate fear must rank as one of the most important discoveries of prehistoric times, along with the use of fire and the first crude stone axe. From prehistoric times to the present, I believe, rape has played a critical function . . . it is nothing more or less than a conscious process of intimidation by which *all* men keep *all* women in a state of fear. (p. 14, emphasis in the original)

Leaving aside the question of how Brownmiller comes by her amazing information about prehistoric psychology, her message is clear: men are inherently rapists.

To back this up, Brownmiller plays fast and loose with anecdotal accounts and passages of fiction, her selection of evidence revealing tremendous bias. At one point she states, "People often ask what the classic Greek myths reveal about rape. Actually, they reveal very little" (p. 313). Yet these myths are widely held to be archetypes of human psychology. If Brownmiller wishes to maintain that there is a continuum of male oppression that extends from man's first recognition of his genitalia as weapon through this very moment she must, in honesty, consider Greek mythology. She can't just pick and choose the evidence that supports her position.

Most women are not raped

Yet even dipping into history and fiction when and where they choose, radical feminists' evidence still doesn't lead to the conclusion that all men are rapists. In the preface to their 1991 book *Acquaintance Rape: The Hidden Crime*, editors Andrea Parrot and Laurie Bechhofer offer a common statistic: "Approximately one in four women in the United States will be the victims of rape or attempted rape by the time they are in their mid-twenties, and over three quarters of those assaults will occur between people who know each other" (p. ix). This stunning figure is supported by FBI records.

In looking at such terrifying statistics, women have a natural tendency to overlook a vital aspect of what is being said: three out of four women will *not* be raped. Even assuming that there is a one-to-one correlation between victims and rapists—a generous assumption, since many rapists commit serial crimes—this means that 75% of all men will never commit this brutal act. Indeed, many men would come immediately to the defense of a woman being attacked.

This observation may seem obvious or facile. But in the face of astounding and unsupported claims like "all men are rapists," it becomes necessary to state the obvious. If another group of radicals claimed that all whites or Protestants or bisexuals were sadists, yet the statistics they provided indicated that at least 75% were not, no honest observer would accept their argument. But when the radicals are sexually correct feminists, their incredible statements are swallowed whole.

And lest a single man try to slip through the net of accusations by pleading that he has never raped or even contemplated doing so, Brownmiller explains how good intentions and good behavior do not excuse a man from the charge of rape.

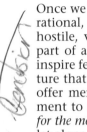

> Once we accept as basic truth that rape is not a crime of irrational, impulsive, uncontrollable lust, but is a deliberate, hostile, violent act of degradation and possession on the part of a would-be conqueror, designed to intimidate and inspire fear, we must look toward those elements in our culture that promote and propagandize these attitudes, which offer men . . . the ideology and psychological encouragement to commit their acts of aggression *without awareness, for the most part, that they have committed a punishable crime,* let alone a moral wrong. (p. 391, emphasis in original)

Such a theory allows for no contradictory evidence. There is no possibility—through action, thought, or word—for a man to escape the charge of rape. It becomes axiomatically true.

The third myth Brownmiller propounds is that rape is part of normal life. Yet her book examines rape primarily during times of war and political crisis. This allows for some valuable scholarship, but it leads to some shaky conclusions. According to Brownmiller, because men rape in times of war and social turbulence, they are normally rapists; rape is the norm.

This requires a leap of logic. The circumstances Brownmiller highlights—war, riots, pogroms, revolutions—are expressions, not of consistent social attitudes, but of social breakdown. Yet in chapter after chapter, Brownmiller uses horrifying accounts of rape from such periods of crisis to make claims about the attitudes and behavior of the ordinary man-on-the-street. Arguing from the extreme, Brownmiller draws conclusions about the normal.

There is no doubt: in times of war and social upheaval, the frequency of all violence increases. But this says nothing about regular life. Nor does it indicate whether the violence is caused by society or by the forces ripping society apart. Men kill in war, but that doesn't make the accountant feeding his parking meter a murderer.

Even when *Against Our Will* moves away from the agonies of war and revolt, it still focuses on situations of polarization and conflict. After the chapters titled "War" and "Riots, Pogroms, and Revolutions" comes "Two Studies in American History." These studies involve the history of rape as applied to American Indians and slaves. Again, Brownmiller offers some valuable insights—but with much narrower application than she is willing to accept.

Redefining rape

Years ago, I watched a television interview in which a Russian sociologist claimed there was no rape in Soviet Russia. Pressed on the point, the woman explained, "No word for rape exists in the Russian language; therefore, there is no rape."

I have no idea whether her linguistic claim is true, but her methodology is familiar: By not naming a problem or reclassifying it, it is supposed to go away. A similar sleight of hand seems to be at work right now, only in reverse. Through a semantic shell game, rape is being redefined out of recognizability.

In their essay, "The Psychology of the Rapist and His Victim," Lilia Melani and Linda Fodaski virtually equate heterosexual sex with rape:

> Once we accept the relationship of aggression and submission; once we recognize force or struggle as an integral component of the sexual courtship (as in the battle of the sexes) it follows that the sex act itself is only a less emphatic expression of all those elements that make up criminal rape. *(Rape: The First Sourcebook for Feminists,* p. 88)

That view is, of course, an extreme. But today's crusade against date rape is well within the feminist mainstream.

Through a semantic shell game, rape is being redefined out of recognizability.

No one can condone rape in the guise of dating. But for many feminists, "date rape"—as a concept—is much more than a stand against drunken frat brothers assaulting female students. In their 1989 book *The Female Fear,* Margaret Gordon and Stephanie Riger come close to denying the possibility of consent within dating itself: "The American dating system, which constitutes a primary source of heterosexual contacts, legitimizes the consensual 'purchase' of women as sexual objects and obliterates the crucial distinction between consent and nonconsent" (p. 60).

It is difficult to tell what constitutes consent or coercion for radical feminists. Consider a recent definition of sexual violence offered by Liz Kelly:

> Sexual violence includes any physical, visual, verbal, or sexual act that is experienced by the woman or girl, at the time or later, as a threat, invasion, or assault, that has the effect of hurting her or degrading her and/or takes away her ability to control intimate contact. *(Surviving Sexual Violence,* 1988, p. 41)

This, in one form or another, has become a common guideline for identifying sexual violence. And it is a dangerous one.

According to this standard, a woman need not have felt threatened during the sex act itself to have been raped. Consider Kelly's words: "Sexual violence includes any . . . sexual act that is experienced by the woman or girl, at the time or *later"* as violent. In retrospect and in light of other experiences, the woman might decide that she had been coerced. But everyone makes mistakes. Regret is not a benchmark of consent.

And how can anything "experienced by the woman or girl" as violent be *de facto* violence—especially when verbal or visual "violence" is included? The crucial link between coercion and the use or threat of force has been broken. Tangible evidence of violence—bruises, witnesses, explicit threats—is no longer needed for a man to be considered guilty. A woman need only *feel* threatened, invaded, or assaulted by him.

Such subjectivity makes a mockery of rule of law. The issue of rape has been legally skewed in favor of the accused for so long that women have reacted by swinging the balance too far in the other direction.

By expanding the definition of rape with such wild abandon, radical feminists have blurred all clear lines on this issue. Rape used to be forced sex—a form of assault. Today, the focus has shifted from assault to "abuse." A recent survey by two Carleton University sociologists, financed by a $236,000 government grant, revealed that 81% of women attending Canadian universities and colleges had suffered sexual abuse. Their survey descended into a maelstrom of controversy when it became known that the researchers defined "abuse" to include taunts and insults during quarrels.

In *Men Who Rape*, Groth provides the essential distinction between rape and sex that occurs under pressure or persuasion: "The defining characteristic of forced assault is the risk of bodily harm to the woman should she refuse to participate in sexual activity. All nonconsenting sex is assault. In the pressured assault, the victim is sexually harassed or exploited. In forced assaults, she is a victim of rape" (p. 3).

By eliminating the distinction between force and persuasion, important sexual lines are erased—such as the line between rape and seduction.

Camille Paglia offers a refreshing contrast to the obfuscations other feminists are weaving around rape:

> [F]eminism, which has waged a crusade for rape to be taken more seriously, has put young women in danger by hiding the truth about sex from them.
>
> In dramatizing the pervasiveness of rape, radical feminists have told young women that before they have sex with a man, they must give consent as explicit as a legal contract's. In this way, young women have been convinced that they have been the victims of rape. *(Sex, Art, and American Culture*, 1992, p. 49)

The pivotal difference between individualist feminists and radical feminists lies in the concepts of coercion and consent. For individualist feminists, these concepts rest on every woman's inalienable right to her own body. If a woman says "yes" (or if her behavior clearly implies "yes"), consent is present. If a woman says "no" (or clearly implies it), coercion is present.

For radical feminists, on the other hand, the distinction is little more than a muddle.

Feminists must accept reality

Radical feminists are trying to create a virtual utopia of safety for women. In Paglia's words, "The point is, these white, upper-middle-class feminists believe that a pain-free world is achievable. I'm saying that a pain-free world will be achievable only under totalitarianism" (p. 64).

But the fact that women are vulnerable to attack means we cannot have it all. We cannot walk at night across an unlit campus without incurring real danger. These are things every woman should be able to do, but "shoulds" of this sort belong in a utopian world. They belong in a world where you drop your wallet in a crowd and have it returned, complete with credit cards and cash; a world in which unlocked Porsches are parked in downtown New York, and children can be left unattended in the park. This is not the reality that confronts and confines us.

Paglia has introduced some reality into the discussion: "Feminism . . . keeps telling women they can do anything, go anywhere, say anything, wear anything. No, they can't. Women will always be in sexual danger. . . . Feminism, with its pie-in-the-sky fantasies about the perfect world, keeps young women from seeing life as it is" (p. 50).

Radical feminism paints a schizoid picture of women. We are supposed to be free and complete sexual beings—who live in a state of siege. We are supposed to be empowered sisters—terrified to open our doors at night. The picture of men is no less confusing: even the kindest, gentlest husband, father, and son is supposed to benefit from the rape of women they love. No ideology that makes such vicious accusations can heal any wounds. It can only provoke hostility.

By eliminating the distinction between force and persuasion, important sexual lines are erased—such as the line between rape and seduction.

This antagonism may serve an unpleasant purpose. Radical feminism is a cry for revolution, and revolutions are not built on conciliation. For radical feminists, there is no solution to sexual violence short of adopting their entire social, economic, and political agenda. No other bridge of understanding or trust may be built between men and women.

Nor does radical feminism seek to help women on an individual basis. Even the supposedly definitive work on rape, *Against Our Will*, gives only a cursory nod to the idea of individual women healing, or learning to defend themselves. Instead, those who have been raped are told that they will never recover from the experience, that rape is the worst thing that can happen to a woman. As Paglia observes, "The whole system now is designed to make you feel that you are maimed and mutilated forever if something like that happens. . . . [T]he whole system is filled with these clichés about sex" (p. 63).

As a woman who has been raped, I will never downplay the trauma it brings. But being raped was not the worst thing that ever happened to me, and I have recovered from it. Feminists who say otherwise are paying me a disrespect.

Consent and coercion

The issue of rape has been diverted into a political tangle of class theory and ideology. It is time to return to the basics: consent and coercion.

So far as consent is concerned, the crucial question must always be, *Has a woman agreed to have sex?* It is not *Has she been talked into it, bribed, manipulated, filled with regret, drunk too much, or ingested drugs?* And in an act that rarely has an explicit "yes" attached to it, the touchstone of consent has to be the presence or absence of physical force.

On the question of coercion, I think feminists desperately need to change their focus from the man to the woman. They should be crying out for every woman to learn how to say "no" as effectively as possible—with deadly force if necessary. The true way to empower a woman, to make her the equal of any man who would attack her, is to teach her to defend herself.

Women *should* be able to live unthreatened by the specter of rape—just as they *should* be able leave their apartments and car doors unlocked. Yet women who bolt their doors every night often refuse to learn self-defense because they don't believe they should have to. Because they *should* be able to feel safe, they refuse to take steps that would so dramatically acknowledge how unsafe they truly are.

Feminism needs more women like Paxton Quigley, author of *Armed and Female*. After a friend of hers was brutally raped, Quigley went from agitating for gun control to teaching women how to use handguns.

In an act that rarely has an explicit "yes" attached to it, the touchstone of consent has to be the presence or absence of physical force.

Quigley uses an effective technique to break through women's tendency to shy away from guns. Her beginner's course includes a tape of a 911 emergency call that was made by a Kansas rape victim as her attacker was breaking into her home. As he appears at her bedroom door, she screams: "Who are you? Why are you here? Why are you here? WHY?"

Once they've heard the tape, Quigley's students are more willing to learn such techniques as how to shoot lying down and how to aim for the head.

If there is a solution to rape and other violence against women, it is self-defense. Politicizing women's pain has been a costly diversion from the hard work necessary to create real safety. As one of the women who took Quigley's course told *The Wall Street Journal*, "Girls grow up believing that they're going to be taken care of, but it just ain't so."

Rape is a crime committed against individual women, and the remedy must be an individualist one as well. Women who are raped deserve one-on-one compassion and respect for the unique suffering they experience. Too much emphasis has been placed on the commonality of reactions among raped women: it is equally important to treat these women as distinct human beings and respect their differences.

By the same token, women in fear deserve one-on-one training in how to defend themselves. Theories of how Neanderthal man was sexist do not offer women safety in their own homes. Women deserve to be empowered, not by having their pain and fear attached to a political agenda, but by learning how to use force to their advantage.

Self-defense is feminism's final frontier.

5

Antirape Activists Exaggerate the Threat of Rape

Katie Roiphe

Katie Roiphe is the author of Last Night in Paradise *and* The Morning After: Sex, Fear, and Feminism on Campus, *from which the following viewpoint is excerpted.*

College antirape demonstrations—such as the annual Take Back the Night marches held on many campuses—have led many people to conclude that rape is a more extensive problem than it actually is. In fact, such activism has encouraged women to blur the distinction between rape and a bad but consensual sexual experience, and in some cases it has prompted false accusations and fabrications of rape. Furthermore, campus antirape activism persuades women to see themselves as helpless victims of male sexual aggression, thereby reinforcing the stereotype that women are weak and vulnerable. Promoting these negative stereotypes and seeking power through victimhood are not constructive ways to combat sexual violence.

It's April—leaves sprouting, flowers, mad crushes, flirtations, Chaucer's pilgrims, bare legs, long days, and marches against rape. Renewal means more than those practically obscene magnolia trees again, branches laden with Georgia O'Keeffe blossoms. Renewal means more than passing exams and drinking wine outside. It means more than enjoying the lengthening day: it means taking back the night.

It's a Saturday night. It's the end of the month and it still hasn't gotten warm. Instead of listening to bands, or watching movies, or drinking beer, more than four hundred Princeton students are "taking back the night." That is, they are marching, as one of the organizers says into the microphone, "to end sexual violence against women." In past years the numbers have climbed to a thousand participants. Carrying candles, the students march through campus, past the library, and down Prospect Street, past the eating clubs, the social hub of Princeton's undergraduates. The marchers chant "Princeton unite, take back the night, Princeton unite, take back the night," and a drumbeat adds drama, noise, and substance to their voices. As they pass the eating clubs the chants get louder, more forceful. "No matter what we wear, no matter where we go, yes means yes and no means no!" It's already dark. They scheduled the march earlier this year, because last year's march went until three in the morning. "Hey ho! Hey ho! Sexism has got to go." As they march, girls put their arms around each other. Some of the march organizers wear armbands. This is to identify them in case anyone falls apart and needs to talk.

"Speaking out" against sexual violence

The ritual is this: at various points in the march everyone stops and gathers around the microphone. Then the "survivors" and occasionally the friends of "survivors" get up to "speak out." One by one they take their place at the microphone, and one by one they tell their story. The stories are intimate accounts of sexual violence, ranging from being afraid on the subway to having been the victim of gang rape and incest.

The marchers stand in Prospect Garden, a flower garden behind the faculty club. A short, plump girl who looks like she is barely out of high school cups her hands around the microphone. Her face is pink from the cold. She begins to describe a party at one of the eating clubs. Her words are slow, loud, deliberate. That night, she had more beers than she could remember, and she was too drunk to know what was going on. A boy she knew was flirting with her, he asked her to go back to his room—it all happened so fast. Her friends told her not to. They told her she was too drunk to make decisions. She went anyway, and he raped her. Later, she says, his roommates thought he was cool for "hooking up." She left her favorite blue jean jacket in his room. She finally went and got it back, but she never wore it again. She pauses. Later the boy apologized to her, so, she says angrily, he must have known it was rape. She stops talking and looks into the crowd. Everyone applauds to show their support.

The stories are intimate accounts of sexual violence, ranging from being afraid on the subway to having been the victim of gang rape and incest.

As the applause dies down, another girl stands up, her face shiny with tears, and brushes the blond hair out of her eyes. I wasn't going to speak out, she explains, because I wasn't a survivor of rape, but I too was silenced. A friend, she continues, someone I used to have a crush on, betrayed my trust. We were lying next to each other and he touched my body. She pauses, swallowing the tears rising in her throat, then goes on: I didn't say anything, I was too embarrassed to say or do anything. I just pretended I was asleep. Distraught, confused, she talks in circles for a while, not sure where her story is leading her, and finally walks away from the microphone.

The next girl to speak out wears a leather jacket and black jeans. People think of me as a bitch, she says, her voice loud, confident, angry, they think of me as a slut. They think I treat men badly. But she explains that underneath her bitchiness is a gang rape that happened when she was sixteen. So if you see someone who acts like me, you shouldn't judge them or hate them, she says. Considering what happened to me I am in good shape, she says, I'm doing really well. It's just fucking great that I can even have orgasms. As she leaves the microphone, her friends put their arms around her.

People stand beneath Blair Arch, the final spot for the speak-outs. The night has gotten cold, but no one seems to notice. Even though baby-sitting has been arranged by the organizers, someone has brought a young child in a stroller. Above the marchers' heads is an open dorm window. Through it, we can hear the sounds of boys watching sports on television. Intermittently the survivors' stories are punctuated by the cheers of these boys—"Yeah!" and "All right!"—when something happens in their game. Their shouts, full of footballs and touchdowns, full of self-consciously virile joy in male strength, provide a strange background for stories about rape. To the marchers below, these shouts are unwitting demonstrations of masculinity at fault. As one boy says into the microphone, "This isn't (and shouldn't be) a good night to be a man."

As these different girls . . . get up to give intensely personal accounts [of rape], all of their stories begin to sound the same.

Actually, nearly half of those present at the march are male. That has been true at Princeton almost every year. Although some may come out of curiosity, most seem to come to show solidarity. A few of the boys get up to say that they are also affected by sexual violence and proceed to tell stories about their girlfriend's being raped. A few talk about their own experiences of being molested as children by older men, but most tell vicarious stories. One boy with long hair and a long trench coat explains his particularly difficult case: he actually looked like a man who had raped his girlfriend, and the first time he kissed her she threw up.

One boy tells his own story about being afraid of sexual violence. He was seven, wandering around a mall, and he noticed that a man was following him, up and down the escalators, in and out of stores. He finally managed to get away, and through this experience, he says, he truly understands the experience of being a woman and being afraid.

A girl tells of being raped by a Frenchman when she was traveling in Europe. Several girls describe sexual violence in distant lands and foreign languages. A few tell of being molested by a relative. Someone tells of being raped in another country *and* being molested by a relative.

A similarity among victims' stories

The strange thing is that as these different girls—tall and short, fat and thin, nervous and confident—get up to give intensely personal accounts, all of their stories begin to sound the same. Listening to a string of them, I hear patterns begin to emerge. The same phrases float through different voices. Almost all of them begin "I wasn't planning to speak out tonight but . . . ," even the ones who had spoken in previous years. They talk about feeling helpless, and feeling guilty. Some talk about hating their bodies. The echoes continue: "I didn't admit it or talk about it." "I was silenced." "I was powerless over my own body."

The catchwords travel across campuses, and across the boundaries between the spoken and written word. In a piece in the most radical of Harvard's feminist magazines, the *Rag,* one student asks, "Why should I have to pay with silence for a crime committed against my body? . . . I want you to know how it feels to be denied your own voice."[1] Voicelessness is a common motif in Take Back the Night speak-outs. In 1988 the *Daily Princetonian* quoted one speaker as saying, "Victims shouldn't be silenced."[2] At Berkeley, students organized a group designed to combat sexual assault called Coalition to Break the Silence.[3] In the *Nassau Weekly,* Jennifer Goode, a Princeton sophomore, writes that Take Back the Night "counteracts the enforced silence of everyday existence. . . . This Saturday night the silence will be broken."[4]

These Princeton women, future lawyers, newspaper reporters, investment bankers, are hardly the voiceless, by most people's definition. But silence is poetic. Being silenced is even more poetic. These days people vie for the position of being silenced, but being silenced is necessarily a construction of the articulate. Once you're talking about being voiceless, you're already talking. The first Take Back the Night march at Princeton was more than ten years ago, and every year they're breaking the silence all over again. The fashionable cloak of silence is more about style than content.

Built into the rhetoric about silence is the image of a malign force clamping its hands over the mouths of victims. This shadowy force takes on many names—patriarchy, men, society—but with such abstract quantities in the formula, it's hard to fathom the meaning behind the metaphor. It doesn't matter, though. Almost all of the victims continue to talk about their silence.

It is the presumption of silence that gives these women the right to speak, that elevates their words above the competitive noise of the university. Silence is the passkey to the empowering universe of the disempowered. Having been silenced on today's campus is the ultimate source of authority.

To be a part of this blanket warmth . . . students are willing to lie.

One of the most scathing condemnations of the longstanding feminist obsession with silence comes from John Irving. In *The World According to Garp,* Irving tells the story of Ellen James, a modern-day Philomela: she was raped at the age of eleven, and her tongue was cut out by the rapist. Much to Garp's dismay, a group of feminists springs up around her, cutting out their own tongue in a gesture of political solidarity. They communicate through notes: "I am an Ellen Jamesian." They hold meetings and take stands. They dedicate themselves to the cause. When Ellen James herself reappears in the novel as an adult, she confesses that she hates the Ellen Jamesians. Beneath his comic, excessive, grotesque image of this feminist clan, Irving makes a realistic point about the feminist pre-occupation with silence. He takes the political reality of feminists' insistence on identification with victims one step further: his feminists are so eager to declare themselves silenced that they are actually willing to cut out their own tongue.

As I listen to the refrains, "I have been silent," "I was silenced," "I am finally breaking the silence," the speakers begin to blur together in my mind. It makes sense that rape victims experience some similar reactions, but what is strange is that they choose the same words. Somehow the individual power of each story is sapped by the collective mode of expression. The individual details fade, the stories blend together, sounding programmed and automatic. As I listen to them I am reminded of the scene in Madeleine L'Engle's children's book *A Wrinkle in Time* in which a row of identical children play outside of a row of identical houses, bouncing a row of identical balls.

The *Rag's* account of a rape ends "Thanks [to] the rest of you for listening," and an account published in the *Daily Princetonian* ends "Thank you for listening."[5] As the vocabulary shared across campuses reveals, there is an archetype, a model, for the victim's tale. Take Back the Night speak-outs follow conventions as strict as any sonnet sequence or villanelle. As intimate details are squeezed into formulaic standards, they seem to be wrought with an emotion more generic than heartfelt.

March as therapy?

One theme that runs through all the speak-outs is self-congratulation—I have survived and now I am to be congratulated. Rhapsodies of self-affirmation may be part of "the healing practice," but as speaker after speaker praises herself for inner strength, they begin to seem excessive. From this spot in American culture, beneath Blair Arch at a Take Back the Night march, the population seems more oversaturated with self-esteem than with cholesterol. One common formulation at Take Back the Night is: "I am a survivor and it's a miracle every time I get a good grade, it's a miracle when I have friends, it's a miracle when I have relationships. It's a miracle. And I thank God every day." In the account in the *Daily Princetonian*, the survivor closes by saying, "If you don't know how to react next time you see me, give me a hug and tell me that you think I'm very brave. Because I, like all the other victims who speak out at Take Back the Night, am very brave."[6]

In the context of Take Back the Night, it is entirely acceptable to praise yourself for bravery, to praise yourself for recovery, and to praise yourself for getting out of bed every morning and eating breakfast. Each story chronicles yet another ascent toward self-esteem, yet another "revolution from within."

As survivors tell their stories, as people hold hands, as they march and chant, there is undoubtedly a cathartic release. There is a current of support between listeners and speakers. At Columbia last year, students waited on line for hours to tell their stories, and as they did the listeners would chant, "It's not your fault," "We believe you," "We love you," and "Tell your story." The energy runs through the applause and the tears, the candlelight and the drumbeats. This is the same energy that sells millions of self-help books every year. This is march as therapy.

In the words of Susan Teres, director of SHARE, Princeton's sexual harassment and assault-education and counseling program, the march is about "finding your own healing practices" and "taking back who you are and what you need and want. This is your journey, your reclaiming of a strong sense of self." The language is New Age mixed with recovery group. At the end of the march there is a moment of silence. Everyone holds hands. Afterward there is a midnight workshop, called Claiming the Vision: A Ritual of Healing and Commitment.

Some feminists argue that Take Back the Night thrusts the issue of safety, more blue lights, and more full-time rape counselors into the public eye. But the march also has its less practical dimension: its ritualistic, symbolic meaning that eclipses the nuts and bolts of specific demands. With its candles, its silence, its promise of transformations, this movement offers a substitute for religion. The symbol of Take Back the Night, emblazoned on T-shirts, buttons, and posters, is three women holding up the moon. All of that moon imagery seems strange, evoking latter-day earth goddesses roaming through Princeton's campus.

Princeton's women's center does run "moon groups" dedicated to the worship of pagan nature goddesses. Jan Strout, director of Princeton's women's center, defines this new feminist spirituality in these terms: "Part of what happens with patriarchy is this whole mind-body split, and it's sort of crazy-making. There's a desire to find a way of wholeness, a way of integration. We try to create new forms of woman-centered or nonhierarchical empowered notions of what it means to have a spiritual essence." Like other movements dealing in spiritual essence, this one is not immune to murky definitions of reality and truth.

False accusations

To be a part of this blanket warmth, this woman-centered nonhierarchical empowered notion, students are willing to lie. My first year at Princeton, one student was caught fabricating a rape story. Mindy had spoken at Take Back the Night for each of her four years at Princeton, and she had printed her story in the *Daily Princetonian*. What's interesting is that her account didn't really stand out; she sounded like everyone else at the speak-out. Her story could have been the blueprint. Whatever else anyone can say about her, Mindy could really talk the talk.

Her story went like this: she left the eating clubs after one boy "started hitting on me in a way that made me feel particularly uncomfortable." He followed her home and "dragged" her back to his room. The entire campus, as she described it, was indifferent: "Although I screamed the entire time, no one called for help, no one even looked out the window to see if the person screaming was in danger." He "carried" her to his room "and, while he shouted the most degrading obscenities imaginable, raped me." He told her that "his father buys him cheap girls like me to use up and throw away." And then he banged her head against the metal bedpost until she was unconscious. She then explained that he was forced to leave campus for a year and now he was back. "Because I see this person every day," she claimed, "my rape remains a constant daily reality for me." Now, she said, she was on the road to recovery, and "there are some nights when I sleep soundly and there are even some mornings when I look in the mirror and I like what I see. I may be a victim, but now I am also a survivor."[7]

Unlike most participants in the speak-outs, Mindy put her story in print. Once it spilled over from the feverish midnight outpouring of the march into black-and-white newsprint, the facts could be checked. The problem was that she claimed she had reported a rape, and she hadn't. She claimed an administrator had told her "to let bygones be bygones," and he hadn't. She told people that a certain male undergraduate was the rapist, and he complained to the administration.

It's impossible to tell how many of these [rape] stories are authentic, faithful accounts of what actually happened.

In May of her senior year, 1991, Mindy came clean. Responding to administrative pressure, she printed an apology for her false accusation in the *Daily Princetonian*. She wrote of the person she accused, "I have never met this individual or spoken to him . . . I urge students who are knowledgeable of this situation to cease blaming this person for my attack."[8] Mindy seemed to explain her motivation for inventing the story as political: "I made my statements in the *Daily Princetonian* and at the Take Back the Night March in order to raise awareness for the plight of the campus rape victims."[9] So these were fictions in the service of political truth.

Mindy also claimed that she was swept up in the heat of the moment. "In several personal conversations and especially at the Take Back the Night March, I have been overcome by emotion. As a result, I was not as coherent or accurate in my recounting of events as a situation as delicate as this demands." If Mindy's political zeal and emotional intensity blurred the truth of her story, one wonders how many other survivors experience a similar blurring.

The accusation is a serious one, and the boy Mindy accused was in a terrible position in the community until she set the record straight. Accusations of rape stick, and in the twisted justice of the grapevine no one is considered innocent until proven guilty. Some may say, as an editorial in the *Daily Princetonian* did, that Mindy's false accusation was "an isolated incident" and shouldn't affect anyone's attitude toward Take Back the Night. Others would go further and claim that the abstract truth in these accusations eclipses the literal falsehood. In a piece about William Kennedy Smith's date-rape trial, Catharine MacKinnon, a prominent feminist law professor, wrote that the truth of a given accusation should be weighed in the larger political balance: "Did this member of a group sexually trained to woman-hating aggression commit this particular act of woman-hating aggression?"[10] That people like MacKinnon are willing to sacrifice individual certainty to politicized group psychology only encourages the Mindys of the world to make up stories.

At George Washington University a few years ago, another student was caught inventing a rape. Mariam, a sophomore who worked in a rape-crisis center, told a story about "two muscular young-looking black males" in "torn dirty clothing" raping a white student. She later admitted to fabricating the story and wrote in a letter of apology that "my goal from the beginning was to call attention to what I perceived to be a serious safety concern for women."[11] As the black student organization at George Washington pointed out, the fabricated rape was not just a lie, but a lie promoting racist stereotypes.

The spectacle of mass confession

The line between fact and fiction is a delicate one when it comes to survivor stories. In the heat of the moment, in the confessional rush of relating graphic details to a supportive crowd, the truth may be stretched, battered, or utterly abandoned. It's impossible to tell how many of these stories are authentic, faithful accounts of what actually happened. They all sound tinny, staged. Each "I am a survivor and I am here to take back the night" seems rehearsed. The context—microphone, hundreds of strangers, applause—puts what one survivor called "deepest darkest secrets" under a voyeuristic spotlight. As they listen to the stories, people cry and hold hands and put their arms around each other. The few moments before someone steps up to the microphone are thick with tension.

As students throw stories of suffering to the waiting crowds, the spiritual cleansing takes on darker undercurrents. The undercurrent is the competition for whose stories can be more Sadean, more incest-ridden, more violent, more like a paperback you can buy at a train station.

Under Blair Arch, a blind girl takes the microphone and says, I have been oppressed by everybody, straights and gays, Catholics, Jews and Protestants. Unless I am imagining it, a ripple of unease runs through the crowd. There is something obscene about this spectacle. This is theater, late-night drama. One earnest male Princeton junior tells me "it was better last year. More moving. There was more crying. Everyone was crying."

Some of these stories may be moving, may be heartfelt and true, but there is something about this context that numbs. Once, over a cup of coffee, a friend told me she had been raped by a stranger with a knife. I was startled. Small, neat, self-contained, she was not someone prone to bursts of self-revelation. She described it, the flash of the knife, the scramble, the exhaustion, the decision to keep her mind blank, the bruises and the police. After she had finished, she quickly resumed her competent, business-as-usual attitude, her toughness, but I could tell how hard it had been for her to tell me. I felt terrible for her. I felt like there was nothing I could say.

Proclaiming victimhood doesn't help project strength.

But an individual conversation is worlds away from the spectacle of mass confession. I find the public demand—and it is a demand—for intimacy strange and unconvincing. Public confidences have a peculiarly aggressive quality. As Wendy Kaminer writes in her book about the recovery movement, "Never have so many known so much about people for whom they cared so little."[12]

Besides the shady element of spectacle, the march itself is headed in the wrong direction. Take Back the Night works against its own political purpose. Although the march is intended to celebrate and bolster women's strength, it seems instead to celebrate their vulnerability. The marchers seem to accept, even embrace, the mantle of victim status. As the speakers describe every fear, every possible horror suffered at the hands of men, the image they project is one of helplessness and passivity. The march elaborates on just how vulnerable women are. Someone tells me that she wanted to say to the male speaker who said "This isn't . . . a good night to be a man" that it wasn't such a good night to be a woman either. *Drained, beleaguered, anxious,* and *vulnerable* are the words women use to describe how they feel as they walk away from the march. But there is a reason they come year after year. There is power to be drawn from declaring one's victimhood and oppression. There is strength in numbers, and unfortunately right now there is strength in being the most oppressed. Students scramble for that microphone, for a chance for a moment of authority. But I wonder if this kind of authority, the coat-tugging authority of the downtrodden, is really worth it.

Betty Friedan stirred up controversy with a bold critique of the rape-crisis movement. She attacked the political efficacy of this victimized and victimizing stance when she wrote, "Obsession with rape, even offering Band-Aids to its victims, is a kind of wallowing in that victim state, that impotent rage, that sterile polarization."[13] *Impotent* and *sterile* are the right words. This is a dead-end gesture. Proclaiming victimhood doesn't help project strength.

Notes

1. *Rag,* May 1991.

2. *Daily Princetonian,* 22 April 1988.

3. *Chronicle of Higher Education,* 17 December 1986.

4. *Nassau Weekly,* 23 April 1992.

5. *Rag,* May 1991; *Daily Princetonian,* 23 April 1991.

6. *Daily Princetonian,* 23 April 1991.

7. Ibid.

8. Ibid., 22 May 1991.

9. Ibid.

10. *New York Times,* 15 December 1991.

11. *Chronicle of Higher Education,* 19 December 1990.

12. Wendy Kaminer, *I'm Dysfunctional, You're Dysfunctional* (Reading, Mass.: Addison-Wesley, 1992), 33.

13. Betty Friedan, *The Second Stage* (New York: Summit Books, 1981), 362.

6

Critics Underestimate the Potential Consequences of Date Rape

Mary Gaitskill

Mary Gaitskill is the author of Bad Behavior, *a collection of short stories, and the novel* Two Girls, Fat and Thin.

Many commentators claim that date rape is not a serious violation and that antirape activists have exaggerated the incidence of and the effects of date rape. Furthermore, these critics charge that some feminist activists belittle women by encouraging them to view themselves as helpless victims of male sexual aggression. While these critics make valid points, they fail to recognize that not everyone processes experience in the same way. Although some women's experiences of sexual violation may not fit the classic definition of forcible rape, this should not discount their emotional pain. To reduce the threat of date rape, women must feel free to address the reasons why they feel sexually victimized.

In the early 1970s, I had an experience that could be described as acquaintance rape. Actually, I have had two or three such experiences, but this one most dramatically fits the profile. I was sixteen and staying in the apartment of a slightly older girl I'd just met in a seedy community center in Detroit. I'd been in her apartment for a few days when an older guy she knew came over and asked us if we wanted to drop some acid. In those years, doing acid with complete strangers was consistent with my idea of a possible good time, so I said yes. When I started peaking, my hostess decided she had to go see her boyfriend, and there I was, alone with this guy, who, suddenly, was in my face.

A sexual violation

He seemed to be coming on to me, but I wasn't sure. My perception was quite loopy, and on top of that he was black and urban-poor, which meant that I, being very inexperienced and suburban-white, did not know how to read him the way I might have read another white kid. I tried to distract him with conversation, but it was hard, considering that I was having trouble with logical sentences, let alone repartee. During one long silence, I asked him what he was thinking. Avoiding my eyes, he answered, "That if I wasn't such a nice guy you could really be getting screwed." The remark sounded to me like a threat, albeit a low-key one. But instead of asking him to explain himself or to leave, I changed the subject. Some moments later, when he put his hand on my leg, I let myself be drawn into sex because I could not face the idea that if I said no, things might get ugly. I don't think he had any idea how unwilling I was—the cultural unfamiliarity cut both ways—and I suppose he may have thought that all white girls just kind of lie there and don't do or say much. My bad time was made worse by his extreme gentleness; he was obviously trying very hard to please me, which, for reasons I didn't understand, broke my heart. Even as inexperienced as I was, I sensed that in his own way he intended a romantic encounter.

The complete truth [about date rape] is more complicated than most of the intellectuals who have written scolding essays on victimism seem willing to accept.

For some time afterward I described this event as "the time I was raped." I knew when I said it that the statement wasn't quite accurate, that I hadn't, after all, said no. Yet it *felt* accurate to me. In spite of my ambiguous, even empathic feelings for my unchosen partner, unwanted sex on acid is a nightmare, and I did feel violated by the experience. At times I even flat-out lied about what had happened, grossly exaggerating the violence and the threat—not out of shame or guilt, but because the pumped-up version was more congruent with my feelings of violation than the confusing facts. Every now and then, in the middle of telling an exaggerated version of the story, I would remember the actual man and internally pause, uncertain of how the memory squared with what I was saying or where my sense of violation was coming from—and then I would continue with my story. I am ashamed to admit this, both because it is embarrassing to me and because I am afraid the admission could be taken as evidence that women lie "to get revenge." I want to stress that I would not have lied that way in court or in any other context that might have had practical consequences; it didn't even occur to me to take my case to court. My lies were told not for revenge but in service of what I felt to be the metaphorical truth.

I remember my experience in Detroit, including its aftermath, every time I hear or read yet another discussion of what constitutes "date rape." I remember it when yet another critic castigates "victimism" and complains that everyone imagines himself or herself to be a victim and that no one accepts responsibility anymore. I could imagine telling my story as a verification that rape occurs by subtle threat as well as by overt force. I could also imagine telling it as if I were one of those crybabies who want to feel like victims. Both stories would be true and not true. The complete truth is more complicated than most of the intellectuals who have written scolding essays on victimism seem willing to accept. I didn't understand my own story fully until I described it to an older woman many years later, as a proof of the unreliability of feelings. "Oh, I think your feelings were reliable," she returned. "It sounds like you were raped. It sounds like you raped yourself." I immediately knew that what she said was true, that in failing even to try to speak up for myself, I had, in a sense, raped myself.

I don't say this in a tone of self-recrimination. I was in a difficult situation: I was very young, and he was aggressive. But my inability to speak for myself—to *stand up* for myself—had little to do with those facts. I was unable to stand up for myself because I had never been taught how.

Conflicting rules

When I was growing up in the 1960s, I was taught by the adult world that good girls never had sex and bad girls did. This rule had clarity going for it but little else; as it was presented to me, it allowed no room for what I actually might feel, what I might want or not want. Within the confines of this rule, I didn't count for much, and I quite vigorously rejected it. Then came the less clear "rules" of cultural trend and peer example that said that if you were cool you wanted to have sex as much as possible with as many people as possible. This message was never stated as a rule, but, considering how absolutely it was woven into the social etiquette of the day (at least in the circles I cared about), it may as well have been. It suited me better than the adults' rule—it allowed me my sexuality, at least—but again it didn't take into account what I might actually want or not want.

The encounter in Detroit, however, had nothing to do with being good or bad, cool or uncool. It was about someone wanting something I didn't want. Since I had been taught only how to follow rules that were somehow more important than I was, I didn't know what to do in a situation where no rules obtained and that required me to speak up on my own behalf. I had never been taught that my behalf mattered. And so I felt helpless, even victimized, without really knowing why.

My parents and my teachers believed that social rules existed to protect me and that adhering to these rules constituted social responsibility. Ironically, my parents did exactly what many commentators recommend as a remedy for victimism. They told me they loved me and that I mattered a lot, but this was not the message I got from the way they conducted themselves in relation to authority and social convention—which was not only that I didn't matter but that *they* didn't matter. In this, they were typical of other adults I knew as well as of the culture around them. When I began to have trouble in school, both socially and academically, a counselor exhorted me to "just play the game"—meaning to go along with everything from school policy to the adolescent pecking order—regardless of what I thought of "the game." My aunt, with whom I lived for a short while, actually burned my jeans and T-shirts because they violated what she understood to be the standards of decorum. A close friend of mine lived in a state of war with her father because of her hippie clothes and hair—which were, of course, de rigueur among her peers. Upon discovering that she was smoking pot, he had her institutionalized.

Many middle-class people—both men and women—were brought up, like I was, to equate responsibility with obeying external rules. And when the rules no longer work, they don't know what to do—much like the enraged, gun-wielding protagonist of the movie *Falling Down*, played by Michael Douglas, who ends his ridiculous trajectory by helplessly declaring, "I did everything they told me to." If I had been brought up to reach my own conclusions about which rules were congruent with my internal experience of the world, those rules would have had more meaning for me. Instead, I was usually given a series of static pronouncements. For example, when I was thirteen, I was told by my mother that I couldn't wear a short skirt because "nice girls don't wear skirts above the knee." I countered, of course, by saying that my friend Patty wore skirts above the knee. "Patty is not a nice girl," returned my mother. But Patty *was* nice. My mother is a very intelligent and sensitive person, but it didn't occur to her to define for me what she meant by "nice," what "nice" had to do with skirt length, and how the two definitions might relate to what I had observed to be nice or not nice—and then let me decide for myself. It's true that most thirteen-year-olds aren't interested in, or much capable of, philosophical discourse, but that doesn't mean that adults can't explain themselves more completely to children. Part of becoming responsible is learning how to make a choice about where you stand in respect to the social code and then holding yourself accountable for your choice. In contrast, many children who grew up in my milieu were given abstract absolutes that were placed before us as if our thoughts, feelings, and observations were irrelevant.

Unspoken assumptions about victims

Recently I heard a panel of feminists on talk radio advocating that laws be passed prohibiting men from touching or making sexual comments to women on the street. Listeners called in to express reactions both pro and con, but the one I remember was a woman who said, "If a man touches me and I don't want it, I don't need a law. I'm gonna beat the hell out of him." The panelists were silent. Then one of them responded in an uncertain voice, "I guess I just never learned how to do that." I understood that the feminist might not want to get into a fistfight with a man likely to be a lot bigger than she, but if her self-respect was so easily shaken by an obscene comment made by some slob on the street, I wondered, how did she expect to get through life? She was exactly the kind of woman whom the cultural critics Camille Paglia and Katie Roiphe have derided as a "rape-crisis feminist"—puritans, sissies, closet-Victorian ladies who want to legislate the ambiguity out of sex. It was very easy for me to feel self-righteous, and I muttered sarcastically at my radio as the panel yammered about self-esteem.

I was conflicted, however. If there had been a time in my own life when I couldn't stand up for myself, how could I expect other people to do it? It could be argued that the grown women on the panel should be more capable than a sixteen-year-old girl whacked out on acid. But such a notion presupposes that people develop at a predictable rate or react to circumstances by coming to universally agreed-upon conclusions. This is the crucial unspoken presumption at the center of the date-rape debate as well as of the larger discourse on victimism. It is a presumption that in a broad but potent sense reminds me of a rule.

Feminists who postulate that boys must obtain a spelled-out "yes" before having sex are trying to establish rules, cut in stone, that will apply to any and every encounter and that every responsible person must obey. The new rule resembles the old good girl/bad girl rule not only because of its implicit suggestion that girls have to be protected but also because of its absolute nature, its iron-fisted denial of complexity and ambiguity. I bristle at such a rule and so do a lot of other people. But should we really be so puzzled and indignant that another rule has been presented? If people have been brought up believing that to be responsible is to obey certain rules, what are they going to do with a can of worms like "date rape" except try to make new rules that they see as more fair or useful than the old ones?

I was unable to stand up for myself because I had never been taught how.

But the "rape-crisis feminists" are not the only absolutists here; their critics play the same game. Camille Paglia, author of *Sexual Personae*, has stated repeatedly that any girl who goes alone into a frat house and proceeds to tank up is cruising for a gang bang, and if she doesn't know that, well, then she's "an idiot." The remark is most striking not for its crude unkindness but for its reductive solipsism. It assumes that all college girls have had the same life experiences as Paglia, and have come to the same conclusions about them. By the time I got to college, I'd been living away from home for years and had been around the block several times. I never went to a frat house, but I got involved with men who lived in rowdy "boy houses" reeking of dirty socks and rock and roll. I would go over, drink, and spend the night with my lover of the moment; it never occurred to me that I was in danger of being gang-raped, and if I had been, I would have been shocked and badly hurt. My experience, though some of it had been bad, hadn't led me to conclude that boys plus alcohol equals gang bang, and I was not naive or idiotic. Katie Roiphe, author of *The Morning After: Fear, Sex, and Feminism on Campus*, criticizes girls who, in her view, create a myth of false innocence: "But did these twentieth-century girls, raised on Madonna videos and the six o'clock news, really trust that people were good until they themselves were raped? Maybe. Were these girls, raised on horror movies and glossy Hollywood sex scenes, really as innocent as all that?" I am sympathetic to Roiphe's annoyance, but I'm surprised that a smart chick like her apparently doesn't know that people process information and imagery (like Madonna videos and the news) with a complex subjectivity that doesn't in any predictable way alter their ideas about what they can expect from life.

Roiphe and Paglia are not exactly invoking rules, but their comments seem to derive from a belief that everyone except idiots interprets information and experience in the same way. In that sense, they are not so different in attitude from those ladies dedicated to establishing feminist-based rules and regulations for sex. Such rules, just like the old rules, assume a certain psychological uniformity of experience, a right way.

Political ploys or emotional truths?

The accusatory and sometimes painfully emotional rhetoric conceals an attempt not only to make new rules but also to codify experience. The "rape-crisis feminists" obviously speak for many women and girls who have been raped or have *felt* raped in a wide variety of circumstances. They would not get so much play if they were not addressing a widespread and real experience of violation and hurt. By asking, "Were they really so innocent?" Roiphe doubts the veracity of the experience she presumes to address because it doesn't square with hers or with that of her friends. Having not felt violated herself—even though she says she has had an experience that many would now call date rape—she cannot understand, or even quite believe, that anyone else would feel violated in similar circumstances. She therefore believes all the fuss to be a political ploy or, worse, a retrograde desire to return to crippling ideals of helpless femininity. In turn, Roiphe's detractors, who have not had her more sanguine "morning after" experience, believe her to be ignorant and callous, or a secret rape victim in deep denial. Both camps, believing their own experience to be the truth, seem unwilling to acknowledge the emotional truth on the other side.

It is at this point that the "date-rape debate" resembles the bigger debate about how and why Americans seem so eager to identify themselves and be identified by others as victims. Book after article has appeared, written in baffled yet hectoring language, deriding the P.C. [politically correct] goody-goodies who want to play victim and the spoiled, self-centered fools who attend twelve-step programs, meditate on their inner child, and study pious self-help books. The revisionist critics have all had a lot of fun with the recovery movement, getting into high dudgeon over those materially well-off people who describe their childhoods as "holocausts" and winding up with a fierce exhortation to return to rationality. Rarely do such critics make any but the most superficial attempt to understand why the population might behave thus.

The "rape-crisis feminists" obviously speak for many women and girls who have been raped or who have felt *raped in a wide variety of circumstances.*

In a fussing, fuming essay in *Harper's Magazine* ("Victims, All?" October 1991) that has almost become a prototype of the genre, David Rieff expressed his outrage and bewilderment that affluent people would feel hurt and disappointed by life. He angrily contrasted rich Americans obsessed with their inner children to Third World parents concerned with feeding their actual children. On the most obvious level, the contrast is one that needs to be made, but I question Rieff's idea that suffering is one definable thing, that he knows what it is, and that since certain kinds of emotional pain don't fit this definition they can't really exist. This idea doesn't allow him to have much respect for other people's experience— or even to see it. It may be ridiculous and perversely self-aggrandizing for most people to describe whatever was bad about their childhood as a "holocaust," but I suspect that when people talk like that they are saying that as children they were not given enough of what they would later need in order to know who they are or to live truly responsible lives. Thus they find themselves in a state of bewildering loss that they can't articulate, except by wild exaggeration—much like I defined my inexplicable feelings after my Detroit episode. "Holocaust" may be a grossly inappropriate exaggeration. But to speak in exaggerated metaphors about psychic injury is not so much the act of a crybaby as it is a distorted attempt to explain one's own experience. I think the distortion comes from a desperate desire to make one's experience have consequence in the eyes of others, and that such desperation comes from a crushing doubt that one's own experience counts at all.

Pain is not easy to codify

In her book *I'm Dysfunctional, You're Dysfunctional*, Wendy Kaminer speaks harshly of women in some twelve-step programs who talk about being metaphorically raped. "It is an article of faith here that suffering is relative; no one says she'd rather be raped metaphorically than in fact," she writes, as if not even a crazy person would prefer a literal rape to a metaphorical one. But actually, I might. About two years after my "rape" in Detroit, I was raped for real. The experience was terrifying: my attacker repeatedly said he was going to kill me, and I thought he might. The terror was acute, but after it was over it actually affected me less than many other mundane instances of emotional brutality I've suffered or seen other people suffer. Frankly, I've been scarred more by experiences I had on the playground in elementary school. I realize that the observation may seem bizarre, but for me the rape was a clearly defined act, perpetrated upon me by a crazy asshole whom I didn't know or trust; it had nothing to do with me or who I was, and so, when it was over, it was relatively easy to dismiss. Emotional cruelty is more complicated. Its motives are often impossible to understand, and it is sometimes committed by people who say they like or even love you. Nearly always it's hard to know whether you played a role in what happened, and, if so, what the role was. The experience *sticks* to you. By the time I was raped I had seen enough emotional cruelty to feel that the rape, although bad, was not especially traumatic.

My response may seem strange to some, but my point is that pain can be an experience that defies codification. If thousands of Americans say that they are in psychic pain, I would not be so quick to write them off as self-indulgent fools. A metaphor like "the inner child" may be silly and schematic, but it has a fluid subjectivity, especially when projected out into the world by such a populist notion as "recovery." Ubiquitous recovery-movement phrases like "We're all victims" and "We're all co-dependent" may not seem to leave a lot of room for interpretation, but they are actually so vague that they beg for interpretation and projection. Such phrases may be fair game for ridicule, but it is shallow to judge them on their face value, as if they hold the same meaning for everyone. What is meant by an "inner child" depends on the person speaking, and not everyone will see it as a metaphor for helplessness. I suspect that most inner-child enthusiasts use the image of themselves as children not so that they can *avoid* being responsible but to learn responsibility by going back to the point in time when they *should* have been taught responsibility—the ability to think, choose, and stand up for themselves—and were not. As I understand it, the point of identifying an "inner child" is to locate the part of yourself that didn't develop into adulthood and then to develop it yourself.

Whether or not this works is an open question, but it is an attempt to accept responsibility, not to flee it.

When I was in my late teens and early twenties, I could not bear to watch movies or read books that I considered demeaning to women in any way; I evaluated everything I saw or read in terms of whether it expressed a "positive image" of women. I was a very P.C. feminist before the term existed, and, by the measure of my current understanding, my critical rigidity followed from my inability to be responsible for my own feelings. In this context, being responsible would have meant that I let myself feel whatever discomfort, indignation, or disgust I experienced without allowing those feelings to determine my entire reaction to a given piece of work. In other words, it would have meant dealing with my feelings and what had caused them, rather than expecting the outside world to assuage them. I could have chosen not to see the world through the lens of my personal unhappiness and yet maintained a kind of respect for my unhappiness. For example, I could have decided to avoid certain films or books because of my feelings without blaming the film or book for making me feel the way I did.

My emotional irresponsibility did not spring from a need to feel victimized, although it may have looked that way to somebody else. I essentially was doing what I had seen most mainstream cultural critics do—it was from them that I learned to view works of art in terms of the message they imparted and, further, that the message could be judged on the basis of consensual ideas about what life is, and how it can and should be seen. My ideas, like most P.C. ideas, were extreme, but they were consistent with more mainstream thought—they just shifted the parameters of acceptability a bit.

[It's taken as an article of faith that] not even a crazy person would prefer a literal rape to a metaphorical one. But actually, I might.

Things haven't changed much: at least half the book and film reviews that I read praise or condemn a work on the basis of the likability of the characters (as if there is a standard idea of what is likable) or because the author's point of view is or is not "life-affirming"—or whatever the critic believes the correct attitude toward life to be. The lengthy and rather hysterical debate about the film *Thelma and Louise*, in which two ordinary women become outlaws after one of them shoots the other's rapist, was predicated on the idea that stories are supposed to function as instruction manuals, and that whether the film was good or bad depended on whether the instructions were correct. Such criticism assumes that viewers or readers need to see a certain type of moral universe reflected back at them or, empty vessels that they are, they might get confused or depressed or something. A respected mainstream essayist writing for *Time* faulted my novel *Two Girls, Fat and Thin* for its nasty male characters, which he took to be a moral statement about males generally. He ended his piece with the fervent wish that fiction not "diminish" men or women but rather seek to "raise our vision of" both—in other words, that it should present the "right" way to the reader, who is apparently not responsible enough to figure it out alone.

I have changed a lot from the P.C. teenager who walked out of movies that portrayed women in a demeaning light. As I've grown older, I've become more confident of myself and my ability to determine what happens to me, and, as a result, those images no longer have such a strong emotional charge. I don't believe they will affect my life in any practical sense unless I allow them to do so. I no longer feel that misogynistic stories are about me or even about women (whether they purport to be or not) but rather are about the kinds of experience the authors wish to render—and therefore are not my problem. I consider my current view more balanced, but that doesn't mean my earlier feelings were wrong. The reason I couldn't watch "disrespect to women" at that time was that such depictions were too close to my own experience (most of which was not unusual), and I found them painful. I was displaying a simplistic self-respect by not subjecting myself to something I was not ready to face. Being unable to separate my personal experience from what I saw on the screen, I was not dealing with my own particular experience—I think, paradoxically, because I hadn't yet learned to value it. It's hard to be responsible for something that isn't valuable. Someone criticizing me as dogmatic and narrow-minded would have had a point, but the point would have ignored the truth of my unacknowledged experience, and thus ignored me.

Emotional truth deserves scrutiny

Many critics of the self-help culture argue against treating emotional or metaphoric reality as if it were equivalent to objective reality. I agree that they are not the same. But emotional truth is often bound up with truth of a more objective kind and must be taken into account. This is especially true of conundrums such as date rape and victimism, both of which often are discussed in terms of unspoken assumptions about emotional truth anyway. Sarah Crichton, in a cover story for *Newsweek* on "Sexual Correctness," described the "strange detour" taken by some feminists and suggested that "we're not creating a society of Angry Young Women. These are Scared Little Girls." The comment is both contemptuous and superficial; it shows no interest in *why* girls might be scared. By such logic, anger implicitly is deemed to be the more desirable emotional state because it appears more potent, and "scared" is used as a pejorative. It's possible to shame a person into hiding his or her fear, but if you don't address the cause of the fear, it won't go away. Crichton ends her piece by saying, "Those who are growing up in environments where they don't have to figure out what the rules should be, but need only follow what's been prescribed, are being robbed of the most important lesson there is to learn. And that's how to live." I couldn't agree more. But unless you've been taught how to think for yourself, you'll have a hard time figuring out your own rules, and you'll feel scared—specially when there is real danger of sexual assault.

Unless you've been taught how to think for yourself, you'll have a hard time figuring out your own rules, and you'll feel scared—especially when there is real danger of sexual assault.

One reason I had sex with strangers when I didn't really want to was that part of me wanted the adventure, and that tougher part ran roughshod over the part of me that was scared and uncertain. I'll bet the same thing happened to many of the boys with whom I had these experiences. All people have their tough, aggressive selves as well as their more delicate selves. If you haven't developed these characteristics in ways that are respectful of yourself and others, you will find it hard to be responsible for them. I don't think it's possible to develop yourself in such ways if you are attuned to following rules and codes that don't give your inner world enough importance. I was a strongwilled child with a lot of aggressive impulses, which, for various reasons, I was actively discouraged from developing. They stayed hidden under a surface of extreme passivity, and when they did appear it was often in a wildly irresponsible, almost crazy way. My early attraction to aggressive boys and men was in part a need to see *somebody* act out the distorted feelings I didn't know what to do with, whether it was destructive or not. I suspect that boys who treat girls with disrespectful aggression have failed to develop their more tender, sensitive side and futilely try to regain it by "possessing" a woman. Lists of instructions about what's nice and what isn't will not help people in such a muddled state, and it's my observation that many people are in such a state to a greater or lesser degree.

I am not idealistic enough to hope that we will ever live in a world without rape and other forms of sexual cruelty; I think men and women will always have to struggle to behave responsibly. But I think we could make the struggle less difficult by changing the way we teach responsibility and social conduct. To teach a boy that rape is "bad" is not as effective as making him see that rape is a violation of his own masculine dignity as well as a violation of the raped woman. It's true that children don't know big words and that teenage boys aren't all that interested in their own dignity. But these are things that children learn more easily by example than by words, and learning by example runs deep.

A few years ago I invited to dinner at my home a man I'd known casually for two years. We'd had dinner and comradely drinks a few times. I didn't have any intention of becoming sexual with him, but after dinner we slowly got drunk and were soon floundering on the couch. I was ambivalent not only because I was drunk but because I realized that although part of me was up for it, the rest of me was not. So I began to say no. He parried each "no" with charming banter and became more aggressive. I went along with it for a time because I was amused and even somewhat seduced by the sweet, junior-high spirit of his manner. But at some point I began to be alarmed, and then he did and said some things that turned my alarm into fright. I don't remember the exact sequence of words or events, but I do remember taking one of his hands in both of mine, looking him in the eyes, and saying, "If this comes to a fight you would win, but it would be very ugly for both of us. Is that really what you want?"

His expression changed and he dropped his eyes; shortly afterward he left.

I consider that small decision to have been a responsible one because it was made by taking both my vulnerable feelings and my carnal impulses into account. When I spoke, my words came from my feeling of delicacy as well as from my capacity for aggression. And I respected my friend as well by addressing both sides of his nature. It is not hard for me to make such decisions now, but it took me a long time to get to this point. I only regret that it took so long, both for my young self and for the boys I was with, under circumstances that I now consider disrespectful to all concerned.

7

Feminist Research Exaggerates the Prevalence of Acquaintance Rape

Christina Hoff Sommers

Christina Hoff Sommers is an associate professor of philosophy at Clark University in Worcester, Massachusetts. She is also the author of Who Stole Feminism? How Women Have Betrayed Women.

Much of the frequently cited research on sexual violence exaggerates the incidence of acquaintance rape. For example, one commonly quoted statistic—that one out of four college women is a victim of rape or attempted rape—is based on research that incorporated misleading and ambiguous questions. Such unsound research—often backed by feminists—has helped to create an overly broad definition of rape that does not take into account whether the woman expressed lack of consent or whether she considered herself a victim of rape. Preventing acquaintance rape will require policies based on accurate information about the prevalence of sexual violence.

I apologize to the reader for my clinical tone. As a crime against the person, rape is uniquely horrible in its long-term effects. The anguish it brings is often followed by an abiding sense of fear and shame. Discussions of the data on rape inevitably seem callous. How can one quantify the sense of deep violation behind the statistics? Terms like *incidence* and *prevalence* are statistical jargon; once we use them, we necessarily abstract ourselves from the misery. Yet, it remains clear that to arrive at intelligent policies and strategies to decrease the occurrence of rape, we have no alternative but to gather and analyze data, and to do so does not make us callous. Truth is no enemy to compassion, and falsehood is no friend.

Some feminists routinely refer to American society as a "rape culture." Yet estimates on the prevalence of rape vary wildly. According to the FBI *Uniform Crime Report,* there were 102,560 reported rapes or attempted rapes in 1990.[1] The Bureau of Justice Statistics estimates that 130,000 women were victims of rape in 1990.[2] A Harris poll sets the figure at 380,000 rapes or sexual assaults for 1993.[3] According to a study by the National Victims Center, there were 683,000 completed forcible rapes in 1990.[4] The Justice Department says that 8 percent of all American women will be victims of rape or attempted rape in their lifetime. The radical feminist legal scholar Catharine MacKinnon, however, claims that "by conservative definition [rape] happens to almost half of all women at least once in their lives."[5]

Who is right? Feminist activists and others have plausibly argued that the relatively low figures of the FBI and the Bureau of Justice Statistics are not trustworthy. The FBI survey is based on the number of cases reported to the police, but rape is among the most underreported of crimes. The Bureau of Justice Statistics National Crime Survey is based on interviews with 100,000 randomly selected women. It, too, is said to be flawed because the women were never directly questioned about rape. Rape was discussed only if the woman happened to bring it up in the course of answering more general questions about criminal victimization. The Justice Department has changed its method of questioning to meet this criticism, so we will know [soon] whether this has a significant effect on its numbers. Clearly, independent studies on the incidence and prevalence of rape are badly needed. Unfortunately, research groups investigating in this area have no common definition of rape, and the results so far have led to confusion and acrimony.

The *Ms.* Report

Of the rape studies by nongovernment groups, the two most frequently cited are the 1985 *Ms.* magazine report by Mary Koss and the 1992 National Women's Study by Dr. Dean Kilpatrick of the Crime Victims Research and Treatment Center at the Medical School of South Carolina. In 1982, Mary Koss, then a professor of psychology at Kent State University in Ohio, published an article on rape in which she expressed the orthodox gender feminist view that "rape represents an extreme behavior but *one that is on a continuum with normal male behavior within the culture*" (my emphasis).[6] Some well-placed feminist activists were impressed by her. As Koss tells it, she received a phone call out of the blue inviting her to lunch with Gloria Steinem.[7] For Koss, the lunch was a turning point. *Ms.* magazine had decided to do a national rape survey on college campuses, and Koss was chosen to direct it. Koss's findings would become the most frequently cited research on women's victimization, not so much by established scholars in the field of rape research as by journalists, politicians, and activists.

Koss and her associates interviewed slightly more than three thousand college women, randomly selected nationwide.[8] The young women were asked ten questions about sexual violation. These were followed by several questions about the precise nature of the violation. Had they been drinking? What were their emotions during and after the event? What forms of resistance did they use? How would they label the event? Koss counted anyone who answered affirmatively to any of the last three questions as having been raped:

8. Have you had sexual intercourse when you didn't want to because a man gave you alcohol or drugs?
9. Have you had sexual intercourse when you didn't want to because a man threatened or used some degree of physical force (twisting your arm, holding you down, etc.) to make you?
10. Have you had sexual acts (anal or oral intercourse or penetration by objects other than the penis) when you didn't want to because a man threatened or used some degree of physical force (twisting your arm, holding you down, etc.) to make you?

Certainly, if you pass out and are molested, one would call it rape. But if you drink and, while intoxicated, engage in sex that you later come to regret, have you been raped?

Koss and her colleagues concluded that 15.4 percent of respondents had been raped, and that 12.1 percent had been victims of attempted rape.[9] Thus, a total of 27.5 percent of the respondents were determined to have been victims of rape or attempted rape because they gave answers that fit Koss's criteria for rape (penetration by penis, finger, or other object under coercive influence such as physical force, alcohol, or threats). However, that is not how the so-called rape victims saw it. Only about a quarter of the women Koss calls rape victims labeled what happened to them as rape. According to Koss, the answers to the follow-up questions revealed that "only 27 percent" of the women she counted as having been raped labeled themselves as rape victims.[10] Of the remainder, 49 percent said it was "miscommunication," 14 percent said it was a "crime but not rape," and 11 percent said they "don't feel victimized."[11]

In line with her view of rape as existing on a continuum of male sexual aggression, Koss also asked: "Have you given in to sex play (fondling, kissing, or petting, but not intercourse) when you didn't want to because you were overwhelmed by a man's continual arguments and pressure?" To this question, 53.7 percent responded affirmatively, and they were counted as having been sexually victimized.

The Koss study, released in 1988, became known as the *Ms.* Report. Here is how the Ms. Foundation characterizes the results: "The *Ms.* project—the largest scientific investigation ever undertaken on the subject—revealed some disquieting statistics, including this astonishing fact: one in four female respondents had an experience that met the legal definition of rape or attempted rape."[12]

The "one in four" figure is incorrect

"One in four" has since become the official figure on women's rape victimization cited in women's studies departments, rape crisis centers, women's magazines, and on protest buttons and posters. Susan Faludi defended it in a *Newsweek* story on sexual correctness.[13] Naomi Wolf refers to it in *The Beauty Myth,* calculating that acquaintance rape is "more common than lefthandedness, alcoholism, and heart attacks."[14] "One in four" is chanted in "Take Back the Night" processions, and it is the number given in the date rape brochures handed out at freshman orientation at colleges and universities around the country.[15] Politicians, from Senator Joseph Biden of Delaware, a Democrat, to Republican Congressman Jim Ramstad of Minnesota, cite it regularly, and it is the primary reason for the Title IV "Safe Campuses for Women" provision of the Violence Against Women Act of 1993, which provides twenty million dollars to combat rape on college campuses.[16]

When Neil Gilbert, a professor at Berkeley's School of Social Welfare, first read the "one in four" figure in the school newspaper, he was convinced it could not be accurate. The results did not tally with the findings of almost all previous research on rape. When he read the study he was able to see where the high figures came from and why Koss's approach was unsound.

He noticed, for example, that Koss and her colleagues counted as victims of rape any respondent who answered "yes" to the question "Have you had sexual intercourse when you didn't want to because a man gave you alcohol or drugs?" That opened the door wide to regarding as a rape victim anyone who regretted her liaison of the previous night. If your date mixes a pitcher of margaritas and encourages you to drink with him and you accept a drink, have you been "administered" an intoxicant, and has your judgment been impaired? Certainly, if you pass out and are molested, one would call it rape. But if you drink and, while intoxicated, engage in sex that you later come to regret, have you been raped? Koss does not address these questions specifically, she merely counts your date as a rapist and you as a rape statistic if you drank with your date and regret having had sex with him. As Gilbert points out, the question, as Koss posed it, is far too ambiguous:

> What does having sex "because" a man gives you drugs or alcohol signify? A positive response does not indicate whether duress, intoxication, force, or the threat of force were present; whether the woman's judgment or control were substantially impaired; or whether the man purposefully got the woman drunk in order to prevent her resistance to sexual advances. . . . While the item could have been clearly worded to denote "intentional incapacitation of the victim," as the question stands it would require a mind reader to detect whether any affirmative response corresponds to this legal definition of rape.[17]

Koss, however, insisted that her criteria conformed with the legal definitions of rape used in some states, and she cited in particular the statute on rape of her own state, Ohio: "No person shall engage in sexual conduct with another person . . . when . . . for the purpose of preventing resistance the offender substantially impairs the other person's judgment or control by administering any drug or intoxicant to the other person" (Ohio revised code 1980, 2907.01A, 2907.02).[18]

Two reporters from the *Blade*—a small, progressive Toledo, Ohio, newspaper that has won awards for the excellence of its investigative articles—were also not convinced that the "one in four" figure was accurate. They took a close look at Koss's study and at several others that were being cited to support the alarming tidings of widespread sexual abuse on college campuses. In a special three-part series on rape called "The Making of an Epidemic," published in October 1992, the reporters, Nara Shoenberg and Sam Roe, revealed that Koss was quoting the Ohio statute in a very misleading way: she had stopped short of mentioning the qualifying clause of the statute, which specifically *excludes* "the situation where a person plies his intended partner with drink or drugs in hopes that lowered inhibition might lead to a liaison."[19] Koss now concedes that question eight was badly worded. Indeed, she told the *Blade* reporters, "At the time I viewed the question as legal; I now concede that it's ambiguous."[20] As Koss herself told the *Blade*, once you remove the positive responses to the alcohol question, the finding that one in seven college women is a victim of rape drops to one in nine.[21] But, as we shall see, this figure too is unacceptably high.

For Gilbert, the most serious indication that something was basically awry in the *Ms.*/Koss study was that the majority of women she classified as having been raped *did not believe they had been raped.* Of those Koss counts as having been raped, only 27 percent thought they had been; 73 percent did not say that what happened to them was rape. In effect, Koss and her followers present us with a picture of confused young women overwhelmed by threatening males who force their attentions on them during the course of a date but are unable or unwilling to classify their experience as rape. Does that picture fit the average female undergraduate? For that matter, does it plausibly apply to the larger community? As the journalist Cathy Young observes, "Women have sex after initial reluctance for a number of reasons . . . fear of being beaten up by their dates is rarely reported as one of them."[22]

Why reject women's judgment?

Katie Roiphe, author of *The Morning After: Sex, Fear, and Feminism on Campus*, argues along similar lines when she claims that Koss had no right to reject the judgment of the college women who didn't think they were raped. But Katha Pollitt of *The Nation* defends Koss, pointing out that in many cases people are wronged without knowing it. Thus we do not say that victims of other injustices—fraud, malpractice, job discrimination— have suffered no wrong as long as they are unaware of the law."[23]

Pollitt's analogy is faulty, however. If Jane has ugly financial dealings with Tom and an expert explains to Jane that Tom has defrauded her, then Jane usually thanks the expert for having enlightened her about the legal facts. To make her case, Pollitt would have to show that the rape victims who were unaware that they were raped would accept Koss's judgment that they really were. But that has not been shown; Koss did not enlighten the women she counts as rape victims, and they did not say "now that you explain it, we can see we were."

Koss and Pollitt make a technical (and in fact dubious) legal point: women are ignorant about what counts as rape. Roiphe makes a straightforward human point: the women were there, and they know best how to judge what happened to them. Since when do feminists consider "law" to override women's experience?

Koss also found that 42 percent of those she counted as rape victims went on to have sex with their attackers on a later occasion. For victims of attempted rape, the figure for subsequent sex with reported assailants was 35 percent. Koss is quick to point out that "it is not known if [the subsequent sex] was forced or voluntary" and that most of the relationships "did eventually break up subsequent to the victimization."[24] But of course, *most* college relationships break up eventually for one reason or another. Yet, instead of taking these young women at their word, Koss casts about for explanations of why so many "raped" women would return to their assailants, implying that they may have been coerced. She ends by treating her subjects' rejection of her findings as evidence that they were confused and sexually naive. There is a more respectful explanation. Since most of those Koss counts as rape victims did not regard themselves as having been raped, why not take this fact and the fact that so many went back to their partners as reasonable indications that they had not been raped to begin with?

The Toledo reporters calculated that if you eliminate the affirmative responses to the alcohol or drugs question, and also subtract from Koss's results the women who did not think they were raped, her one in four figure for rape and attempted rape "drops to between one in twenty-two and one in thirty-three."[25]

The National Women's Study

The other frequently cited nongovernment rape study, the National Women's Study, was conducted by Dean Kilpatrick. From an interview sample of 4,008 women, the study projected that there were 683,000 rapes in 1990. As to prevalence, it concluded that "in America, one out of every eight adult women, or at least 12.1 million American women, has been the victim of forcible rape sometime in her lifetime."[26]

Unlike the Koss report, which tallied rape attempts as well as rapes, the Kilpatrick study focused exclusively on rape. Interviews were conducted by phone, by female interviewers. A woman who agreed to become part of the study heard the following from the interviewer: "Women do not always report such experiences to police or discuss them with family or friends. The person making the advances isn't always a stranger, but can be a friend, boyfriend, or even a family member. Such experiences can occur anytime in a woman's life—even as a child."[27] Pointing out that she wants to hear about any such experiences "regardless of how long ago it happened or who made the advances," the interviewer proceeds to ask four questions:

1. Has a man or boy ever made you have sex by using force or threatening to harm you or someone close to you? Just so there is no mistake, by sex we mean putting a penis in your vagina.
2. Has anyone ever made you have oral sex by force or threat of harm? Just so there is no mistake, by oral sex we mean that a man or boy put his penis in your mouth or somebody penetrated your vagina or anus with his mouth or tongue.
3. Has anyone ever made you have anal sex by force or threat of harm?
4. Has anyone ever put fingers or objects in your vagina or anus against your will by using force or threat?

Any woman who answered yes to any one of the four questions was classified as a victim of rape. This seems to be a fairly straightforward and well-designed survey that provides a window into the private horror that many women, especially very young women, experience. One of the more disturbing findings of the survey was that 61 percent of the victims said they were seventeen or younger when the rape occurred.

There is, however, one flaw that affects the significance of Kilpatrick's findings. An affirmative answer to any one of the first three questions does reasonably put one in the category of rape victim. The fourth is problematic, for it includes cases in which a boy penetrated a girl with his finger, against her will, in a heavy petting situation. Certainly the boy behaved badly. But is he a rapist? Probably neither he nor his date would say so. Yet, the survey classifies him as a rapist and her as a rape victim.

I called Dr. Kilpatrick and asked him about the fourth question. "Well," he said, "if a woman is forcibly penetrated by an object such as a broomstick, we would call that rape."

"So would I," I said. "But isn't there a big difference between being violated by a broomstick and being violated by a finger?" Dr. Kilpatrick acknowledged this: We should have split out fingers versus objects," he said. Still, he assured me that the question did not significantly affect the outcome. But I wondered. The study had found an epidemic of rape among teenagers—just the age group most likely to get into situations like the one I have described.

The more serious worry is that Kilpatrick's findings, and many other findings on rape, vary wildly unless the respondents are explicitly asked whether they have been raped. In 1993, Louis Harris and Associates did a telephone survey and came up with quite different results. Harris was commissioned by the Commonwealth Fund to do a study of women's health. As we shall see, their high figures on women's depression and psychological abuse by men caused a stir.[28] But their finding on rape went altogether unnoticed. Among the questions asked of its random sample population of 2,500 women was, "In the last five years, have you been a victim of a rape or sexual assault?" Two percent of the respondents said yes; 98 percent said no. Since attempted rape counts as sexual assault, the combined figures for rape and attempted rape would be 1.9 million over five years or 380,000 for a single year. Since there are approximately twice as many attempted rapes as completed rapes, the Commonwealth/Harris figure for completed rapes would come to approximately 190,000. That is dramatically lower than Kilpatrick's finding of 683,000 *completed forcible rapes.*

The majority of women [Koss] classified as having been raped did not believe they had been raped.

The Harris interviewer also asked a question about acquaintance and marital rape that is worded very much like Kilpatrick's and Koss's: "In the past year, did your partner ever try to, or force you to, have sexual relations by using physical force, such as holding you down, or hitting you, or threatening to hit you, or not?"[29] Not a single respondent of the Harris poll's sample answered yes.

How to explain the discrepancy? True, women are often extremely reluctant to talk about sexual violence that they have experienced. But the Harris pollsters had asked a lot of other awkward personal questions to which the women responded with candor: 6 percent said they had considered suicide, 5 percent admitted to using hard drugs, 10 percent said they had been sexually abused when they were growing up. I don't have the answer, though it seems obvious to me that such wide variances should make us appreciate the difficulty of getting reliable figures on the risk of rape from the research. That the real risk should be known is obvious. The *Blade* reporters interviewed students on their fears and found them anxious and bewildered. "It makes a big difference if it's one in three or one in fifty," said April Groff of the University of Michigan, who says she is "very scared." "I'd have to say, honestly, I'd think about rape a lot less if I knew the number was one in fifty."[30]

When the *Blade* reporters asked Kilpatrick why he had not asked women whether they had been raped, he told them there had been no time in the thirty-five-minute interview. "That was probably something that ended up on the cutting-room floor."[31] But Kilpatrick's exclusion of such a question resulted in very much higher figures. When pressed about why he omitted it from a study for which he had received a million-dollar federal grant, he replied, "If people think that is a key question, let them get their own grant and do their own study."[32]

Kilpatrick had done an earlier study in which respondents were explicitly asked whether they had been raped. That study showed a relatively low prevalence of 5 percent—one in twenty—and it got very little publicity.[33] Kilpatrick subsequently abandoned his former methodology in favor of the *Ms.*/Koss method, which allows the surveyor to decide whether a rape occurred. Like Koss, he used an expanded definition of rape (both include penetration by a finger). Kilpatrick's new approach yielded him high numbers (one in eight), and citations in major newspapers around the country. His graphs were reproduced in *Time* magazine under the heading, "Unsettling Report on an Epidemic of Rape."[34] Now he shares with Koss the honor of being a principal expert cited by media, politicians, and activists.

Other researchers report low figures for rape

There are many researchers who study rape victimization, but their relatively low figures generate no headlines. The reporters from the *Blade* interviewed several scholars whose findings on rape were not sensational but whose research methods were sound and were not based on controversial definitions. Eugene Kanin, a retired professor of sociology from Purdue University and a pioneer in the field of acquaintance rape, is upset by the intrusion of politics into the field of inquiry: "This is highly convoluted activism rather than social science research."[35] Professor Margaret Gordon of the University of Washington did a study in 1981 that came up with relatively low figures for rape (one in fifty). She tells of the negative reaction to her findings: "There was some pressure—at least I felt pressure—to have rape be as prevalent as possible. . . . I'm a pretty strong feminist, but one of the things I was fighting was that the really avid feminists were trying to get me to say that things were worse than they really are."[36] Dr. Linda George of Duke University also found relatively low rates of rape (one in seventeen), even though she asked questions very close to Kilpatrick's. She told the *Blade* she is concerned that many of her colleagues treat the high numbers as if they are "cast in stone."[37] Dr. Naomi Breslau, director of research in the psychiatry department at the Henry Ford Health Science Center in Detroit, who also found low numbers, feels that it is important to challenge the popular view that higher numbers are necessarily more accurate. Dr. Breslau sees the need for a new and more objective program of research: "It's really an open question. . . . We really don't know a whole lot about it."[38]

Kilpatrick's findings, and many other findings on rape, vary wildly unless the respondents are explicitly asked whether they have been raped.

An intrepid few in the academy have publicly criticized those who have proclaimed a "rape crisis" for irresponsibly exaggerating the problem and causing needless anxiety. Camille Paglia claims that they have been especially hysterical about date rape: "Date rape has swelled into a catastrophic cosmic event, like an asteroid threatening the earth in a fifties science-fiction film."[39] She bluntly rejects the contention that "'No' always means no. . . . 'No' has always been, and always will be, part of the dangerous, alluring courtship ritual of sex and seduction, observable even in the animal kingdom."[40]

Paglia's dismissal of date rape hype infuriates campus feminists, for whom the rape crisis is very real. On most campuses, date-rape groups hold meetings, marches, rallies. Victims are "survivors," and their friends are "co-survivors" who also suffer and need counseling.[41] At some rape awareness meetings, women who have not yet been date raped are referred to as "potential survivors." Their male classmates are "potential rapists."[42]

Has date rape in fact reached critical proportions on the college campus? Having heard about an outbreak of rape at Columbia University, Peter Hellman of *New York* magazine decided to do a story about it.[43] To his surprise, he found that campus police logs showed no evidence of it whatsoever. Only two rapes were reported to the Columbia campus police in 1990, and in both cases, charges were dropped for lack of evidence. Hellman checked the figures at other campuses and found that in 1990 fewer than one thousand rapes were reported to campus security on college campuses in *the entire country*.[44] That works out to fewer than one-half of one rape per campus. Yet despite the existence of a rape crisis center at St. Luke's-Roosevelt Hospital two blocks from Columbia University, campus feminists pressured the administration into installing an expensive rape crisis center inside the university. Peter Hellman describes a typical night at the center in February 1992: "On a recent Saturday night, a shift of three peer counselors sat in the Rape Crisis Center—one a backup to the other two. . . . Nobody called; nobody came. As if in a firehouse, the three women sat alertly and waited for disaster to strike. It was easy to forget these were the fading hours of the eve of Valentine's Day."[45]

In *The Morning After*, Katie Roiphe describes the elaborate measures taken to prevent sexual assaults at Princeton. Blue lights have been installed around the campus, freshman women are issued whistles at orientation. There are marches, rape counseling sessions, emergency telephones. But as Roiphe tells it, Princeton is a very safe town, and whenever she walked across a deserted golf course to get to classes, she was more afraid of the wild geese than of a rapist. Roiphe reports that between 1982 and 1993 only two rapes were reported to the campus police. And, when it comes to violent attacks in general, male students are actually more likely to be the victims. Roiphe sees the campus rape crisis movement as a phenomenon of privilege: these young women have had it all, and when they find out that the world can be dangerous and unpredictable, they are outraged:

> Many of these girls [in rape marches] came to Princeton from Milton and Exeter. Many of their lives have been full of summers in Nantucket and horseback-riding lessons. These are women who have grown up expecting fairness, consideration, and politeness.[46]

Funds for rape prevention are poorly allocated

The *Blade* story on rape is unique in contemporary journalism because the authors dared to question the popular feminist statistics on this terribly sensitive problem. But to my mind, the important and intriguing story they tell about unreliable advocacy statistics is overshadowed by the even more important discoveries they made about the morally indefensible way that public funds for combatting rape are being allocated. Schoenberg and Roe studied Toledo neighborhoods and calculated that women in the poorer areas were nearly thirty times more likely to be raped than those in the wealthy areas. They also found that campus rape rates were thirty times lower than the rape rates for the general population of eighteen- to twenty-four-year-olds in Toledo. The attention and the money are disproportionately going to those least at risk. According to the *Blade* reporters:

> Across the nation, public universities are spending millions of dollars a year on rapidly growing programs to combat rape. Videos, self-defense classes, and full-time rape educators are commonplace, . . . But the new spending comes at a time when community rape programs—also dependent on tax dollars—are desperately scrambling for money to help populations at much higher risk than college students.[47]

One obvious reason for this inequity is that feminist advocates come largely from the middle class and so exert great pressure to protect their own. To render their claims plausible, they dramatize themselves as victims—survivors or "potential survivors." Another device is to expand the definition of rape (as Koss and Kilpatrick do). Dr. Andrea Parrot, chair of the Cornell University Coalition Advocating Rape Education and author of *Sexual Assault on Campus*, begins her date rape prevention manual with the words, "Any sexual intercourse without mutual desire is a form of rape. Anyone who is psychologically or physically pressured into sexual contact on any occasion is *as much a victim* as the person who is attacked in the streets" (my emphasis).[48] By such a definition, privileged young women in our nation's colleges gain moral parity with the real victims in the community at large. Parrot's novel conception of rape also justifies the salaries being paid to all the new personnel in the burgeoning college date rape industry. After all, it is much more pleasant to deal with rape from an office in Princeton than on the streets of downtown Trenton.

Another reason that college women are getting a lion's share of public resources for combatting rape is that collegiate money, though originally public, is allocated by college officials. As the *Blade* points out:

> Public universities have multi-million dollar budgets heavily subsidized by state dollars. School officials decide how the money is spent, and are eager to address the high-profile issues like rape on campus. In contrast, rape crisis centers—nonprofit agencies that provide free services in the community—must appeal directly to federal and state governments for money.[49]

Schoenberg and Roe describe typical cases of women in communities around the country—in Madison, Wisconsin, in Columbus, Ohio, in Austin, Texas, and in Newport, Kentucky—who have been raped and have to wait months for rape counseling services. There were three rapes reported to police at the University of Minnesota in 1992; in New York City there were close to three thousand. Minnesota students have a twenty-four-hour rape crisis hot line of their own. In New York City, the "hot line" leads to detectives in the sex crimes unit. The *Blade* reports that the sponsors of the Violence Against Women Act of 1993 reflect the same bizarre priorities: "If Senator Biden has his way, campuses will get at least twenty million more dollars for rape education and prevention." In the meantime, Gail Rawlings of the Pennsylvania Coalition Against Rape complains that the bill guarantees nothing for basic services, counseling, and support groups for women in the larger community: "It's ridiculous. This bill is supposed to encourage prosecution of violence against women, [and] one of the main keys is to have support for the victim. . . . I just don't understand why [the money] isn't there."[50]

No matter how you look at it, women on campus do not face anywhere near the same risk of rape as women elsewhere.

Because rape is the most underreported of crimes, the campus activists tell us we cannot learn the true dimensions of campus rape from police logs or hospital reports. But as an explanation of why there are so few known and proven incidents of rape on campus, that won't do. Underreporting of sexual crimes is not confined to the campus, and wherever there is a high level of *reported* rape—say in poor urban communities where the funds for combatting rape are almost nonexistent—the level of underreported rape will be greater still. No matter how you look at it, women on campus do not face anywhere near the same risk of rape as women elsewhere. The fact that college women continue to get a disproportionate and ever-growing share of the very scarce public resources allocated for rape prevention and for aid to rape victims underscores how disproportionately powerful and *self-preoccupied* the campus feminists are despite all their vaunted concern for "women" writ large.

Once again we see what a long way the New Feminism has come from Seneca Falls. The privileged and protected women who launched the women's movement, as Elizabeth Cady Stanton and Susan B. Anthony took pains to point out, did not regard *themselves* as the primary victims of gender inequity: "They had souls large enough to feel the wrongs of others without being scarified in their own flesh." They did not act as if they had "in their own experience endured the coarser forms of tyranny resulting from unjust laws, or association with immoral and unscrupulous men."[51] Ms. Stanton and Ms. Anthony concentrated their efforts on the Hester Vaughns and the other defenseless women whose need for gender equity was urgent and unquestionable.

The effects of inflated rape statistics

Much of the unattractive self-preoccupation and victimology that we find on today's campuses has been irresponsibly engendered by the inflated and scarifying "one in four" statistic on campus rape. In some cases the campaign of alarmism arouses exasperation of another kind. In an article in the *New York Times Magazine*, Katie Roiphe questioned Koss's figures: "If 25 percent of my women friends were really being raped, wouldn't I know it?"[52] She also questioned the feminist perspective on male/female relations: "These feminists are endorsing their own utopian vision of sexual relations: sex without struggle, sex without power, sex without persuasion, sex without pursuit. If verbal coercion constitutes rape, then the word rape itself expands to include any kind of sex a woman experiences as negative."[53]

The publication of Ms. Roiphe's piece incensed the campus feminists. "The *New York Times* should be shot," railed Laurie Fink, a professor at Kenyon College.[54] "Don't invite [Katie Roiphe] to your school if you can prevent it," counseled Pauline Bart of the University of Illinois.[55] Gail Dines, a women's studies professor and date rape activist from Wheelock College, called Roiphe a traitor who has sold out to the "white male patriarchy."[56]

Other critics, such as Camille Paglia and Berkeley professor of social welfare Neil Gilbert, have been targeted for demonstrations, boycotts, and denunciations. Gilbert began to publish his critical analyses of the *Ms.*/Koss study in 1990.[57] Many feminist activists did not look kindly on Gilbert's challenge to their "one in four" figure. A date rape clearinghouse in San Francisco devotes itself to "refuting" Gilbert; it sends out masses of literature attacking him. It advertises at feminist conferences with green and orange fliers bearing the headline STOP IT, BITCH! The words are not Gilbert's, but the tactic is an effective way of drawing attention to his work. At one demonstration against Gilbert on the Berkeley campus, students chanted, "Cut it out or cut it off," and carried signs that read, KILL NEIL GILBERT![58] Sheila Kuehl, the director of the California Women's Law

Center, confided to readers of the *Los Angeles Daily Journal,* "I found myself wishing that Gilbert, himself, might be raped and . . . be told, to his face, it had never happened."[59]

The findings being cited in support of an "epidemic" of campus rape are the products of advocacy research. Those promoting the research are bitterly opposed to seeing it exposed as inaccurate. On the other hand, rape is indeed the most underreported of crimes. We need the truth for policy to be fair and effective. If the feminist advocates would stop muddying the waters we could probably get at it.

Is America a "rape culture"?

High rape numbers serve the gender feminists by promoting the belief that American culture is sexist and misogynist. But the common assumption that rape is a manifestation of misogyny is open to question. Assume for the sake of argument that Koss and Kilpatrick are right and that the lower numbers of the FBI, the Justice Department, the Harris poll, of Kilpatrick's earlier study, and the many other studies mentioned earlier are wrong. Would it then follow that we are a "patriarchal rape culture"? Not necessarily. American society is exceptionally violent, and the violence is not specifically patriarchal or misogynist. According to International Crime Rates, a report from the United States Department of Justice, "Crimes of violence (homicide, rape, and robbery) are four to nine times more frequent in the United States than they are in Europe. The U.S. crime rate for rape was . . . roughly seven times higher than the average for Europe."[60] The incidence of rape is many times lower in such countries as Greece, Portugal, or Japan—countries far more overtly patriarchal than ours.

It might be said that places like Greece, Portugal, and Japan do not keep good records on rape. But the fact is that Greece, Portugal, and Japan are significantly less violent than we are. I have walked through the equivalent of Central Park in Kyoto at night. I felt safe, and I was safe, not because Japan is a feminist society (it is the opposite), but because crime is relatively rare. The international studies on violence suggest that patriarchy is not the primary cause of rape but that rape, along with other crimes against the person, is caused by whatever it is that makes our society among the most violent of the so-called advanced nations.

Believing what women actually say is precisely not *the methodology by which some feminist advocates get their incendiary statistics.*

But the suggestion that criminal violence, not patriarchal misogyny, is the primary reason for our relatively high rate of rape is unwelcome to gender feminists like Susan Faludi, who insist, in the face of all evidence to the contrary, that "the highest rate of rapes appears in cultures that have the highest degree of gender inequality, where sexes are segregated at work, that have patriarchal religions, that celebrate all-male sporting and hunting rituals, i.e., a society such as us."[61]

In the spring of 1992, Peter Jennings hosted an ABC special on the subject of rape. Catharine MacKinnon, Susan Faludi, Naomi Wolf, and Mary Koss were among the panelists, along with John Leo of *U.S. News & World Report.* When MacKinnon trotted out the claim that 25 percent of women are victims of rape, Mr. Leo replied, "I don't believe those statistics. . . . That's totally false."[62] MacKinnon countered, "That means you don't believe women. It's not cooked, it's interviews with women by people who believed them when they said it. That's the methodology."[63] The accusation that Leo did not believe "women" silenced him, as it was meant to. But as we have seen, believing what women actually say is precisely *not* the methodology by which some feminist advocates get their incendiary statistics.

Notes

1. Federal Bureau of Investigation, *Crime in the United States: Uniform Crime Reports* (Washington, D.C.: U.S. Department of Justice, 1990).

2. Bureau of the Census, *Statistical Abstract of the United States 1990* (Washington, D.C.: U.S. Government Printing Office, 1992), p. 184. See also Caroline Wolf Harlow, Bureau of Justice Statistics, "Female Victims of Violent Crime" (Washington, D.C.: U.S. Department of Justice, 1991), p. 7.

3. Louis Harris and Associates, "Commonwealth Fund Survey of Women's Health" (New York: Commonwealth Fund, 1993), p. 9. What the report says is that "within the last five years, 2 percent of women (1.9 million) were raped."

4. "Rape in America: A Report to the Nation" (Charleston, S.C.: Crime Victims Research and Treatment Center, 1992).

5. Catharine MacKinnon, "Sexuality, Pornography, and Method," *Ethics* 99 (January 1989): 331.

6. Mary Koss and Cheryl Oros, "Sexual Experiences Survey: A Research Instrument Investigating Sexual Aggression and Victimization," *Journal of Consulting and Clinical Psychology* 50, no. 3 (1982): 455.

7. Nara Schoenberg and Sam Roe, "The Making of an Epidemic," *Blade,* October 10, 1993, special report, p. 4.

8. The total sample was 6,159, of whom 3,187 were females. See Mary Koss, "Hidden Rape: Sexual Aggression and Victimization in a National Sample of Students in Higher Education," in Ann Wolbert Burgess, ed., *Rape and Sexual Assault,* vol. 2 (New York: Garland Publishing, 1988), p. 8.

9. Ibid., p. 10.

10. Ibid., p. 16.

11. Mary Koss, Thomas Dinero, and Cynthia Seibel, "Stranger and Acquaintance Rape," *Psychology of Women Quarterly* 12 (1988): 12. See also Neil Gilbert, "Examining the Facts: Advocacy Research Overstates the Incidence of Date and Acquaintance Rape," in *Current Controversies in Family Violence,* ed. Richard Gelles and Donileen Loseke (Newbury Park, Calif.: Sage Publications, 1993), pp. 120–32.

12. The passage is from Robin Warshaw, in her book *I Never Called It Rape* (New York: HarperPerennial, 1988), p. 2, published by the Ms. Foundation and with an afterword by Mary Koss. The book summarizes the findings of the rape study.

13. *Newsweek,* October 25, 1993.

14. Naomi Wolf, *The Beauty Myth: How Images of Beauty Are Used Against Women* (New York: Doubleday, 1992), p. 166.

15. At the University of Minnesota, for example, new students receive a booklet called "Sexual Exploitation on Campus." The booklet informs them that according to "one study [left unnamed] 20 to 25 percent of all college women have experienced rape or attempted rape."

16. The Violence Against Women Act of 1993 was introduced to the Senate by Joseph Biden on January 21, 1993. It is sometimes referred to as the "Biden Bill." It is now making its way through the various congressional committees. Congressman Ramstad told the Minneapolis *Star Tribune* (June 19, 1991), "Studies show that as many as one in four women will be the victim of rape or attempted rape during her college career." Ramstad adds, "This may only be the tip of the iceberg, for 90 percent of all rapes are believed to go unreported."

17. Gilbert, "Examining the Facts," pp. 120–32.

18. Cited in Koss, "Hidden Rape," p. 9.

19. *Blade,* special report, p. 5.

20. Ibid.

21. Koss herself calculated the new "one in nine" figure for the *Blade,* p. 5.

22. Cathy Young, *Washington Post* (National Weekly Edition), July 29, 1992, p. 25.

23. Katha Pollitt, "Not Just Bad Sex," *New Yorker,* October 4, 1993, p. 222.

24. Koss, "Hidden Rape," p. 16.

25. *Blade,* p. 5. The *Blade* reporters explain that the number varies between one in twenty-two and one in thirty-three depending on the amount of overlap between groups.

26. "Rape in America," p. 2.

27. Ibid., p. 15.

28. The secretary of health and human services, Donna Shalala, praised the poll for avoiding a "white male" approach that has "for too long" been the norm in research about women. My own view is that the interpretation of the poll is flawed.

29. Louis Harris and Associates, "The Commonwealth Fund Survey of Women's Health," p. 20.

30. *Blade,* p. 3.

31. Ibid., p. 6.

32. Ibid.

33. Dean Kilpatrick et al., "Mental Health Correlates of Criminal Victimization: A Random Community Survey," *Journal of Consulting and Clinical Psychology* 53, 6 (1985).

34. *Time,* May 4, 1992, p. 15.

35. *Blade,* special report, p. 3.

36. Ibid., p. 3.

37. Ibid., p. 5.

38. Ibid., p. 3.

39. Camille Paglia, "The Return of Carry Nation," *Playboy,* October 1992, p. 36.

40. Camille Paglia, "Madonna I: Anomility and Artifice," *New York Times,* December 14, 1990.

41. Reported in Peter Hellman, "Crying Rape: The Politics of Date Rape on Campus," *New York,* March 8, 1993, pp. 32–37.

42. *Washington Times,* May 7, 1993.

43. Hellman, "Crying Rape," pp. 32–37.

44. Ibid., p. 34.

45. Ibid., p. 37.

46. Katie Roiphe, *The Morning After: Sex, Fear, and Feminism on Campus* (Boston: Little, Brown, 1993), p. 45.

47. *Blade,* p. 13.

48. Andrea Parrot, *Acquaintance Rape and Sexual Assault Prevention Training Manual* (Ithaca, N.Y.: College of Human Ecology, Cornell University, 1990), p. 1.

49. *Blade,* p. 13.

50. Ibid., p. 14.

51. Alice Rossi, ed., *The Feminist Papers: From Adams to de Beauvoir* (New York: Columbia University Press, 1973), p. 414.

52. Katie Roiphe, "Date Rape's Other Victim," *New York Times Magazine,* June 13, 1993, p. 26.

53. Ibid., p. 40.

54. Women's Studies Network (Internet: LISTSERVE@UMDD.UMD.EDU), June 14, 1993.

55. Ibid., June 13, 1993.

56. See Sarah Crichton, "Sexual Correctness: Has It Gone Too Far?" *Newsweek,* October 25, 1993, p. 55.

57. See Neil Gilbert, "The Phantom Epidemic of Sexual Assault," *The Public Interest,* Spring 1991, pp. 54–65; Gilbert, "The Campus Rape Scare," *Wall Street Journal,* June 27, 1991, p. 10; and Gilbert, "Examining the Facts," pp. 120–32.

58. "Stop It Bitch," distributed by the National Clearinghouse on Marital and Date Rape, Berkeley, California. (For thirty dollars they will send you "thirty-four years of research to help refute him [Gilbert].") See also the *Blade,* p. 5.

59. Sheila Kuehl, "Skeptic Needs Taste of Reality Along with Lessons About Law," *Los Angeles Daily Journal,* September 5, 1991. Ms. Kuehl, it will be remembered, was a key figure in disseminating the tidings that men's brutality to women goes up 40 percent on Super Bowl Sunday. Some readers may remember Ms. Kuehl as the adolescent girl who played the amiable Zelda on the 1960s "Dobie Gillis Show."

60. *International Crime Rates* (Washington, D.C.: Bureau of Justice Statistics, 1988), p. 1. The figures for 1983: England and Wales, 2.7 per 100,000; United States, 33.7 per 100,000 (p. 8). Consider these figures comparing Japan to other countries (rates of rape per 100,000 inhabitants):

	FORCIBLE RAPE
U.S.	38.1
U.K. (England and Wales only)	12.1
(West) Germany	8.0
France	7.8
Japan	1.3

Source: *Japan 1992: An International Comparison* (Tokyo: Japan Institute for Social and Economic Affairs, 1992), p. 93.

61. "Men, Sex, and Rape," ABC News Forum with Peter Jennings, May 5, 1992, Transcript no. ABC-34, p. 21.

62. Ibid., p. 11.

63. Ibid.

8

Feminist Research Does Not Exaggerate the Prevalence of Acquaintance Rape

John K. Wilson

John K. Wilson is author of The Myth of Political Correctness: The Conservative Attack on Higher Education, *from which this viewpoint is taken.*

Several commentators have criticized the frequently cited studies that report a relatively high incidence of acquaintance rape. Critics argue that these feminist-backed studies have defined rape too broadly and have led the public to erroneously believe that date rape has reached epidemic proportions on college campuses. However, these commentators often ignore important aspects of the rape studies they criticize and end up distorting and misrepresenting the results of those studies. Their denial of the realities of date rape is part of a recent backlash against feminism and liberal political ideals.

On the afternoon of 19 April 1988, a nineteen-year-old student at East Stroudsburg State University in Pennsylvania walked to her boyfriend's dormitory. While waiting for him, she went to the dorm room of a friend and encountered his roommate, Robert Berkowitz. When Berkowitz asked her to "hang out for a while," she agreed, but she refused his request to give him a back rub or sit on his bed, saying she didn't trust him.

After talking for a while, Berkowitz got off the bed, sat next to her, and leaned against her until her back was on the floor. Berkowitz straddled her and started kissing her. She said, "Look, I gotta go," saying she had to meet her boyfriend. Berkowitz lifted her shirt and started fondling her. She said, "No." Berkowitz, still on top of her, continued kissing and fondling her for thirty seconds, and she continued to say "no." Berkowitz undid his pants. She kept saying "no" but reports she "really couldn't move" because he was shifting his body on top of her. She said, "No, I gotta go, let me go."

76

Berkowitz went to the door and locked it. He put her on the bed and straddled her again, removing her sweatpants and underwear, and she reports that she "couldn't like go anywhere." She didn't scream because "it was like a dream was happening or something." He started having sex with her and she said "no, no" repeatedly. After about thirty seconds, Berkowitz got off her and said, "Wow, I guess we just got carried away." She said, "No, we didn't get carried away, you got carried away."

Berkowitz was charged with rape, found guilty by a jury, and sentenced to one to four years in prison. But on 27 May 1994, the Pennsylvania Supreme Court overturned the jury's guilty verdict and ruled that what Berkowitz did was not rape because there was no "forcible compulsion" involved.[1]

Between 1988 and 1994, when the rape happened and when the Pennsylvania Supreme Court decided it didn't, a sexual revolution occurred. Anita Hill testified before the Senate Judiciary Committee investigating Clarence Thomas and raised public awareness about "that sexual harassment crap," as Senator Alan Simpson (R-Wyoming) put it.[2] Colleges and universities wrote new policies prohibiting sexual harassment and sexual assault, and began educating students about date rape. Antioch College, in Yellow Springs, Ohio, developed a much-ridiculed policy requiring not just consent but an active "yes" before sexual activity.

A backlash against feminism

But a growing backlash against feminism condemned the increased attention to acquaintance rape and sexual harassment as "a neo-puritan preoccupation" with "a nostalgia for 1950's-style dating" that infantilized women, as Katie Roiphe wrote in a *New York Times* op-ed piece she later expanded into *The Morning After: Sex, Fear, and Feminism on Campus.* Roiphe further claimed that "these feminists are promoting the view of women as weak-willed, alabaster bodies, whose virtue must be protected from the cunning encroachments of the outside world."[3]

A sister phrase to *political correctness* was discovered in a 1993 *Newsweek* cover story: "Sexual Correctness." According to *Newsweek,* because of sexual correctness "verbal coercion can now constitute rape," and feminists are making women into "Scared Little Girls" who are "huddling in packs."[4] But like political correctness, sexual correctness is a media invention with little basis in reality. No men are being thrown in jail for verbal coercion. No women are being weakened by so-called victim feminism. No "sexually correct" dogma reigns on college campuses.

If there is a feminist conspiracy taking over universities and redefining rude behavior as date rape, it is hard to find any evidence of it. On the contrary, most colleges continue to follow the same old policies of denial and dismissal. Katie Koestner was raped in her dormitory room at the College of William and Mary in Williamsburg, Virginia, when she was a freshman. She did not receive a medical examination for twenty-four hours. Rather than filing criminal charges, she was encouraged to use an administrative hearing. At the hearing, it was determined that the rape did not deserve "severe punishment," so the rapist was allowed to remain on campus on the condition that he not enter anyone's living quarters. The college administrator who heard the case told Koestner, "I did find him guilty but I talked to him for a couple of hours this morning and I think he is a good guy. . . . You two should work through this little tiff and get back together next semester."[5] Koestner eventually transferred to another university.[6]

Many colleges are reluctant to take strong action against rape for fear that it will lead to negative publicity. Since all colleges are required to report the number of sexual assaults that occur on campus, many administrators find it more convenient to ignore rape than to encourage women to report it. Brigham Young University, after reported rapes in Provo, Utah, quadrupled, refused to allow a rape-awareness speaker on campus because the subject was "too controversial."[7] Acquaintance rape is sometimes not even recorded by campus police as a crime. One police officer reported that a theft on campus was automatically recorded, but rapes were not listed as crimes "unless the rapist was a total stranger or the victim is in the intensive-care unit."[8] Colleges sometimes respond to a rape by trying to get the victim to leave campus. When Professor Joyce Honeychurch was raped in her office at the University of Alaska, the university offered her a settlement if she would leave.[9]

The refusal to acknowledge the reality of acquaintance rape has terrible consequences for its victims. While all rape victims suffer and many have difficulty recovering from the crime, victims of acquaintance rape are taught to believe that they must have been responsible, which makes the experience even more traumatic. Although acquaintance rape victims suffer the same degree of psychological harm from the rape, they are much less likely than victims of stranger rape to report what happened to the police or tell someone else about it.[10]

Acquaintance rape on college campuses can be particularly traumatic for the victims since they know they may cross paths with their attackers. Two researchers on rape "have heard story after story of individuals transferring or dropping out of school altogether after an assault. It is also apparent from our research that a person is much more likely to transfer or to drop out if the college has failed to take her allegations seriously." They add, "We have heard of cases in which the victim is not permitted to press charges at all, either through the criminal justice system or through the campus judicial hearing process."[11] After complaints from victims that college officials had steered them away from the courts, Connecticut passed a law in 1991 making it a crime for universities to interfere with a student's right to report a crime to police.[12]

If there is a feminist conspiracy taking over universities and redefining rude behavior as date rape, it is hard to find any evidence of it.

The rape myths that permeate the *Berkowitz* case are not limited to the court system; they are also reflected in the current backlash against the women's movement. According to Camille Paglia, the *Berkowitz* case "isn't even remotely about rape" because a woman is "sending a signal" when she "sits on the floor with her breasts sticking up."[13] Paglia claims that "rape has become a joke" and asserts that going to a man's room alone "is in effect consenting to sex." Like the feminists she attacks, Paglia admits that "sex is dangerous" and that "rape is one of the risk factors in getting involved with men."[14] Ironically, it is Paglia who advocates neo-Puritanical standards when she says that a woman who allows herself to be alone in a room with a man is only getting what she deserves if she is raped. No feminist urges returning to the paternalistic age of early curfew for women, open doors, and one-foot-on-the-floor rules. Instead, feminists demand that sexuality must exist in a climate free of violence.

Attacks on feminist research

The most influential attacks on the feminist critique of acquaintance rape have come from Neil Gilbert, a professor of social welfare at Berkeley infamous for telling one of his classes, "Comparing real rape to date rape is like comparing cancer to the common cold."[15] Gilbert has frequently attacked "radical feminists" for doing "advocacy studies" that show what he calls a "phantom epidemic" of rape. Gilbert focuses on a 1985 study by Mary Koss of 3,187 college women, the most extensive research done on the prevalence of rape. Koss found that 27.1 percent had been victims of rape (15.3 percent) or attempted rape (11.8 percent). Koss's study also showed that 84 percent of the victims knew their attacker and that 57 percent of the rapes happened on dates, suggesting that acquaintance rape is widespread.[16] This survey is the source of the common "one-in-four" statistic that Gilbert dismisses as "nonsense-type numbers."[17]

Gilbert notes that of the ten questions asked in the Koss study, most referred to the threat or use of "some degree of physical force"; Gilbert does not dispute them. But two questions, he claims, were "awkward and vaguely worded": "Have you had a man attempt sexual intercourse (get on top of you, attempt to insert his penis) when you didn't want to by giving you alcohol or drugs, but intercourse did not occur? Have you had sexual intercourse when you didn't want to because a man gave you alcohol or drugs?"[18]

However, only 8 percent of the women in the survey said that they had had sexual intercourse because a man had given them alcohol or drugs, a low level considering the frequency of alcohol use in unwanted intercourse. By contrast, 9 percent of the women had had sexual intercourse and 6 percent anal or oral intercourse because "a man threatened or used some degree of physical force (twisting your arm, holding you down, etc.)."[19] It is difficult to imagine anyone quibbling with the wording of these questions (and Gilbert is notably silent about them), since the physical force is explicit and the acts are clearly rape according to legal definitions. At most, Gilbert's challenge to the "alcohol or drugs" question reduces the number of women who had been raped from 15.3 percent to 10.6 percent, and the victims of attempted rape from 11.7 percent to 8.4 percent.[20] Even if all the women who responded to this question were not raped (and some of them certainly were by Gilbert's definition), the proportion of college women who have been victims of rape or attempted rape would decline only from one in four (27.0 percent) to one in five (19.0 percent)—a figure far above the levels Gilbert is willing to admit could be accurate.[21]

Unable to show bias in the questions, Gilbert turns to what the victims themselves said about the incidents. Of those classified as victims of rape, 27 percent said it was rape. Another 14 percent described it as a "crime, but not rape." Only 11 percent said that they didn't "feel victimized," while 49 percent called it "miscommunication."[22] Gilbert distorts this data by claiming that "seventy-three percent of those whom the researcher defined as having been raped did not perceive of themselves as victims."[23] Certainly the women who called it a crime and the respondents who called it miscommunication (without saying they were not raped) refused to describe themselves as not having been victimized.

Gilbert claims that "to deny that a woman would know whether she had been raped says essentially that women are feebleminded."[24] But many women have been taught to believe that acquaintance rape is not rape at all, but merely a bad experience. One study found that women whom Koss categorized as rape victims but who did not themselves call it rape were much more likely than women who called their experience rape to define rape as a physical attack by a stranger.[25] Clearly, one reason why women who are raped do not call it rape is because of their narrow definition of *rape*, not because they were not victims of a sexual assault.

There is no evidence that Koss categorized lesser forms of sexual victimization as rape. Since Koss had separate categories for sexual coercion—where women who "didn't want to" have sexual intercourse were "overwhelmed by a man's continual arguments and pressure" (25 percent of the women surveyed)—it seems doubtful that the cases described by Koss as rape were instead coercion, since respondents had an opportunity to describe an act of sexual victimization as something less serious than being physically forced to have sex.

Gilbert ignores another part of Koss's data, which shows that 84 percent of the women who were raped tried to reason with the attacker, 70 percent put up some form of physical resistance, and 64 percent were held down.[26] If only 27 percent of these women were "really" raped, why did so many more women react as they would in "real" rapes? This contradicts Gilbert's explanation that "later regrets" or male "sweet talk" had been redefined as rape.[27] Gilbert wrongly thinks that feminists "label every bad experience a woman has with a man as rape."[28]

Koss's research is confirmed by other studies

Koss's conclusion that one in four college women have been raped or have faced an attempt at rape is confirmed by other studies that did not include the questions Gilbert challenges. A 1991 survey of women at Purdue found that 17 percent reported being victims of rape or attempted rape, with 69 percent of the attacks made by acquaintances.[29] A survey at the University of South Dakota found that 20.6 percent of women were "physically forced by a dating partner to have sexual intercourse." A similar study at Cornell discovered that 19 percent had experienced "intercourse against their will . . . through rough coercion, threats, force or violence," but only 2 percent said they were raped.[30]

Koss's study is also confirmed by the 1993 National Health and Social Life Survey (NHSLS) conducted by the National Opinion Research Center, the most accurate and comprehensive survey of sex in America to date. The NHSLS found that 22 percent of women have been forced to do something sexually by a man since puberty, and 30 percent of them by more than one man.[31] And even this number underestimates the true level of sexual violence in our society: "Because forced sex is undoubtedly underreported in surveys because of the socially stigmatized nature of the event, we believe that our estimates are probably conservative 'lower-bound' estimates of forced sex within the population."[32]

Victims of acquaintance rape are taught to believe that they must have been responsible, which makes the experience even more traumatic.

The NHSLS found that 25 percent of women aged eighteen to twenty-four had been forced to do something sexually. In more than three quarters of the cases, it was someone the woman knew well (22 percent), was in love with (46 percent), or married to (9 percent)—only 4 percent of the women had been attacked by a stranger.[33] The prevalence of attacks on young women found by Koss is also confirmed by the 1992 "Rape in America" study by the Justice Department, which found that girls under age eighteen were the victims in 61.6 percent of rapes.[34] A 1994 report by the Alan Guttmacher Institute found that 23 percent of fourteen-year-olds are sexually experienced, and 60 percent of their first experiences were coerced.[35]

The NHSLS researchers also explain why they did not ask respondents about forced sex by using the word *rape:* "We purposely did not use the term rape in asking about forced sex, reasoning that there is a fundamental difference between what most people mean when they use the word and what police, prosecutors, and judges will accept in court as legal rape. In addition, the word has strong emotional connotations that may make some women reluctant to apply it in situations they were in, although they may have felt that they were forced to have sex."[36] The NHSLS researchers recognize that the use of the word *rape is* a barrier to getting accurate numbers about sexual violence. In a culture where stranger rape is defined as "real rape," few women are willing to call sexual assault by its real name.

Gilbert criticizes the Koss study by pointing out that "42% of the women who were defined as having been raped had sex again with the men who had supposedly raped them," arguing that in these cases it could not have been rape.[37] Gilbert claims, "Rape is a brutal crime. If you were raped, why would you sleep with your rapist again?"[38] But the facts do not conform to how Gilbert thinks women should act. The NHSLS survey asked respondents about their first act of intercourse and found that 4.2 percent of women were forced the first time they had sex (an additional 24.5 percent did not want to have sex but were not forced). Like the Koss study, this survey determined that a large number of the women forced to have sex (35.7 percent) had intercourse with their attacker again—and half of these women had sex with him at least ten more times.[39] For a variety of reasons, many women do not leave the men who rape them, just as many battered women do not leave their attackers.

Gilbert also claims that the Koss survey must be wrong because of the "tremendous gap" between its results and those from the National Crime Survey (NCS) conducted by the Bureau of Justice Statistics. He notes that the NCS shows that rape and attempted rape fell by 30 percent between 1978 and 1988, with a current rate of 1.2 rapes per 1,000 women.[40] However, Gilbert doesn't mention that the NCS figures he cites are based on a survey that never directly asked about rape (the question supposed to elicit rape responses asked, "Did anyone TRY to attack you in some other way?").[41] These official statistics are so unreliable that the estimate of rapes went from 130,260 in 1990 to 207,610 in 1991, even though there was obviously not a 50 percent increase in rapes in one year.[42]

Those who disagree with Gilbert are never treated as sincere researchers; instead they are said to be part of a feminist, man-hating conspiracy, which uses "advocacy numbers" to "alter consciousness" and falsifies data "not through outright deceit but through a more subtle process of distortion." Gilbert claims that these "radical feminists" want "the feminist-prescribed social inoculation of every woman" because they are "disaffected" women with an "ax to grind"; thus, "Advocacy numbers on sexual assault may resonate with their feelings of being, not literally raped, but figuratively 'screwed over' by men."[43]

In an article on "scientific fraud," Gilbert even accuses Koss of "a misrepresentation of findings to the public" and a deliberate, "breathtaking disregard for the facts" in order to "make them more compatible with the author's conclusion."[44] But Koss's indisputable conclusion is that "the great majority of rape victims conceptualized their experience in highly negative terms and felt victimized whether or not they realized that legal standards for rape had been met."[45] Like any survey on a controversial topic, Koss's study deserves criticism and debate. But Gilbert's depiction of an intellectual opponent as an academic fraud is typical of the extreme efforts to construct the myth of sexual correctness.

The rape deniers insult women

Although Gilbert has done no original research on the subject and shows gross ignorance of basic statistical methodology (he thinks that the biased National Crime Survey is more accurate than Koss's study simply because it used "much larger samples"), he is the most widely known critic of the date rape surveys.[46] Gilbert's critiques of Koss's survey have appeared in leading magazines and national newspapers, and they are treated as gospel by the opponents of the movement against date rape. His "refutation" of the date rape crisis is cited by other attacks on feminism such as Katie Roiphe's *The Morning After* and Christina Hoff Sommers's *Who Stole Feminism?*, both of which use Gilbert's critique as their primary source when they attack the Koss survey.[47] And the distortions multiply as they trickle down: after reading Roiphe's book, Mary Matalin concluded, in a *Newsweek* article, that 73 percent of the victims "affirmed they had intercourse when they didn't want to because a man gave them drugs or alcohol. Warping the statistics trivializes the far fewer but *real* cases of acquaintance rape."[48] In this amazing warping of the statistics (less than a third of the rape victims responded to this question, not 73 percent), Koss's data are assumed to reflect the mistakes of women who got a little too drunk.

Roiphe concludes that Gilbert's arguments show that the question of rape is "a matter of opinion" and "there is a gray area in which someone's rape may be another person's bad night." But rape is a matter of opinion only if you believe that being forced to have sex is a "bad night." Like Paglia and Gilbert, Roiphe sees a conspiracy against sexual desire in the attacks on date rape: "Somebody is 'finding' this rape crisis, and finding it for a reason." The real aim of these feminists, Roiphe tells us, is not to stop rape but to "call into question all relationships between men and women."[49] In the mythical world of sexual correctness, the fight to stop violence against women is perceived as just a feminist conspiracy to destroy men.

Clearly, one reason why women who are raped do not call it rape is because of their narrow definition of rape, not because they were not victims of a sexual assault.

The rape deniers also attack rape surveys on the grounds that they convey (in Gilbert's words) "a view of women as helpless victims."[50] But accurately reporting violence against women does not mean that feminists see women as helpless victims. Certainly not all women are victims of rape, and even those who are should not be depicted as helpless. Contrary to what the rape deniers believe, the cause of women is not promoted by denying the truth about sexual violence. While there is always a danger that reporting the alarming levels of victimization may cause women to be viewed as victims who need to be "protected" by limiting their freedom, this must not lead us to deny the truth. It is a far greater insult to women when the rape deniers depict them as hysterical man bashers who invent charges of rape and suffer from delusional fears.

"Inappropriate innuendo" and other rape myths

In many cases, ridiculous definitions of rape are promoted by the media to show the "extremism" of the antirape movement even though no feminist supports them. A *Chicago Tribune* headline asked, "Should Regretted Sex Be Classified as Date Rape?" as if any feminist actually believed that it ever should.[51] Katie Roiphe writes, "People have asked me if I have ever been date-raped. And thinking back on complicated nights, on too many glasses of wine, on strange and familiar beds, I would have to say yes. With such a sweeping definition of rape, I wonder how many people there are, male or female, who haven't been date-raped at one point or another. People pressure and manipulate and cajole each other into all sorts of things all the time."[52] But it is Roiphe, not a feminist, who gives rape such a sweeping definition.

In 1990, *U.S. News & World Report* columnist John Leo wrote an alarming article about the redefinition of rape: "Driven by feminist ideology, we have constantly extended the definition of what constitutes illicit male behavior. Very ambiguous incidents are now routinely flattened out into male predation and firmly listed under date rape. In Swarthmore College's rape prevention program, 'inappropriate innuendo' is actually regarded as an example of acquaintance rape."[53] Leo's anecdote about Swarthmore seems to be a powerful indictment of radical feminism. But in reality, as Jon Wiener reveals in a *Nation* article, it just isn't true.

The phrase appeared in 1985 when a two-page discussion guide written by a student was sent out with a video to teach students about acquaintance rape. One sentence in the guide declared, "Acquaintance rape as will be discussed spans a spectrum of incidents and behaviors ranging from crimes legally defined as rape to verbal harassment and inappropriate innuendo." But this guide was never given to students and was never endorsed as official Swarthmore policy or the policy of its rape prevention program. Moreover, the statement in the guide was not a feminist redefinition of rape but a poorly written effort to point out that workshops should not be limited to date rape and might encompass a wider range of behavior. Jan Boswinkel, the student who wrote the guide, told Wiener: "I didn't mean to equate innuendo with rape when I wrote that guide."[54] Although a dean and a public relations assistant had unequivocally told a *U.S. News* fact checker that the statement did not represent Swarthmore policy, Leo chose to print the false information not just once but twice, claiming that Swarthmore's policy "comes from open distaste for heterosexual sex" and would "ruin sex for the next generation."[55]

In a culture where stranger rape is defined as "real rape," few women are willing to call sexual assault by its real name.

The anecdote soon took on a life of its own and began popping up in story after story. A 1991 *Time* article on date rape says that "a Swarthmore College training pamphlet once explained that acquaintance rape 'spans a spectrum of incidents and behaviors, ranging from crimes legally defined as rape to verbal harassment and inappropriate innuendo.'"[56] The "inappropriate innuendo" lie was repeated in *Playboy, Time* (again), *Reason*, the *Washington Times* (twice), the *Detroit News and Free Press, Campus*, John Taylor's infamous article in *New York* magazine (reprinted in *Reader's Digest)*, and a syndicated column by *San Jose Mercury News* writer Joanne Jacobs titled "Rape by Innuendo."[57] As Wiener notes, "The story demonstrates that several of America's mainstream publications, with tens of millions of readers, have no shame about using and reusing the same discredited quote as long as it serves an antifeminist political agenda."[58]

But the "innuendo is rape" story is not simply the product of the backlash against feminism. It is also a part of the broader attack on political correctness, in which simple facts are willfully twisted beyond recognition to serve a noble lie in the culture war against radicals of all kinds. The attacks on "rape crisis feminists" fit neatly into this larger culture war, in which the backlash against feminism merges with the myth of political correctness to create the phantom called "sexual correctness."

Notes

1. *Commonwealth v. Berkowitz*, 609 A.2d 1338 (Pa. Super. 1992), 641 A.2d 1161 (Pa. 1994).

2. Karen Branan, "Out for Blood," *Ms.*, January–February 1994, 83.

3. Katie Roiphe, *The Morning After: Sex, Fear, and Feminism on Campus* (Boston: Little, Brown, 1993), 67.

4. Sarah Crichton, "Sexual Correctness: Has It Gone Too Far?" *Newsweek* 25 October 1993, 52–56.

5. Carol Bohmer and Andrea Parrot, *Sexual Assault on Campus* (New York: Macmillan, 1993), 12.

6. Terry Steinberg, "Rape on College Campuses: Reform Through Title IX," *Journal of College and University Law* 18 (1991), 47.

7. Jon Wiener, "God and Man at Hillsdale," *Nation*, 24 February 1992, 236.

8. Carolyn Palmer, "Skepticism Is Rampant about the Statistics on Campus Crime," *Chronicle of Higher Education*, 21 April 1993, B2.

9. Bohmer and Parrot, 60.

10. Mary Koss, Thomas Dinero, Cynthia Seibel, and Susan Cox, "Stranger and Acquaintance Rape: Are There Differences in the Victim's Experience?" *Psychology of Women Quarterly* 12 (1988), 21–22.

11. Bohmer and Parrot, 41, 51.

12. Kathryn Kranhold and Katherine Farrish, "Anxiety about Sex, Dating, Rape Transforms College Life," *Hartford Courant*, 10 October 1993, A1.

13. Nancy Roman, "Scales of Justice Weigh Tiers of Sexual Assault," *Washington Times*, 16 June 1994, A8.

14. Camille Paglia, on Later with Bob Costas, 21 September 1992; Camille Paglia, *Sex, Art, and American Culture* (New York: Vintage, 1992), 68, 63.

15. Kathleen Hendrix, "Defining Controversy," *Los Angeles Times*, 9 July 1991, E1. In criticizing "feminist" research, Gilbert and his supporters, like many critics of political correctness, have adopted the mantle of self-anointed victimhood. Gilbert called a protest against his articles "an attempt to impose a politically correct view." See Virginia Matzek, "Rape Article Sparks Vigil," *Daily Californian*, 19 June 1991. Dean Specht said, "I'm beginning to feel that I'm being victimized" and suggested that Gilbert was "a victim of 'political correctness.'" See Jackie Stevens, "UC School of Social Welfare Still Reeling from Rape Statistics Flap," *Berkeley Express*, 8 November 1991; Harry Specht, letter, 30 July 1991. Yet it is Gilbert's defenders, not the feminists, who are intolerant of opposing views. Paul Terrell, coordinator of academic programs, invited Diane Russell to deliver the 1991 Seabury Lecture. But when Russell indicated that she planned to criticize Gilbert's writings in part of her speech, Terrell replied that the lecture had to be "a decorous, scholarly event" and that "it would be inappropriate for the Seabury lecture to become a critique of Professor Gilbert's work" (letter to Diane Russell, 13 September 1991). Dean Harry Specht admits he ordered the invitation to Russell rescinded, but he reinstated her lecture after students protested his decision.

16. Mary Koss, Christine Gidycz, and Nadine Wisniewski, "The Scope of Rape: Incidence and Prevalence of Sexual Aggression and Victimization

in a National Sample of Higher Education Students," *Journal of Consulting and Clinical Psychology* 55:2 (1987), 162–70.

17. Abby Cohn, "Rape Figures Are Inflated, Professor Says," *Woodland Hills Daily News*, 1 June 1991.

18. Neil Gilbert, "Realities and Mythologies of Rape," *Society*, May–June 1992, 4–5.

19. Koss, Gidycz, and Wisniewski, 167.

20. Christina Hoff Sommers erroneously claimed that "once you remove the positive responses to question eight, the finding that one in four college women is a victim of rape or attempted rape drops to one in nine;" see Sommers, *Who Stole Feminism? How Women Have Betrayed Women* (New York: Simon & Schuster, 1994), 213.

21. See Gilbert, 4–10.

22. Gilbert, 5.

23. Neil Gilbert, "The Phantom Epidemic of Sexual Assault," *Public Interest*, Spring 1991, 60.

24. Carol Brydolf, "Professor: Rape Figures Are Inflated," *Oakland Tribune*, 30 May 1991, A1.

25. See Arnold Kahn, Virginia Mathie, and Cyndee Torgler, "Rape Scripts and Rape Acknowledgment," *Psychology of Women Quarterly* 18 (1994), 60.

26. Mary Koss, "Hidden Rape," in Ann Wolbert Burgess, ed., *Rape and Sexual Assault II* (New York: Garland, 1988),16; Robin Warshaw, *I Never Called It Rape* (New York: Harper & Row, 1988), 49. By contrast, only 26 percent of the women who were "sexually coerced" physically resisted, and only 9 percent said they were held down.

27. Neil Gilbert, "The Campus Rape Scare," *Wall Street Journal*, 27 June 1991.

28. Neil Gilbert, "Counterpoint: A Few Women Want to Speak for Both Sexes," *San Francisco Chronicle*, 26 June 1991.

29. Lyn Kathlene, "Beneath the Tip of the Iceberg," *Women's Review of Books*, February 1992, 30.

30. Susan Estrich, *Real Rape* (Cambridge: Harvard University Press, 1987), 112.

31. Edward Laumann, John Gagnon, Robert Michael, and Stuart Michaels, *The Social Organization of Sexuality* (Chicago: University of Chicago Press, 1994), 337; Gina Kolata, Edward Laumann, John Gagnon, and Robert Michael, *Sex in America: A Definitive Study* (Boston: Little, Brown, 1994), 225.

32. Laumann et al., 322.

33. Laumann et al., 337, 226–27.

34. "Report Cites Heavy Toll of Rapes on Young," *New York Times*, 23 June 1994, A8.

35. "Sexually Active Girls Cite Coercion," *Chicago Tribune*, 8 June 1994,17.

36. Kolata et al., 220.

37. Gilbert, "The Phantom Epidemic of Sexual Assault," 60.

38. Michele N.-K. Collison, "A Berkeley Scholar Clashes with Feminists over Validity of Their Research on Date Rape," *Chronicle of Higher Education,* 26 February 1992, A35–A37, A37; see also Collison, "Article's Attack on 'Hype' Surrounding Date Rape Stirs Debate among Researchers, Campus Counselors," *Chronicle of Higher Education,* 7 July 1993, A41.

39. Laumann et al., 329, 333.

40. Gilbert, "Realities and Mythologies of Rape," 9.

41. See Helen Eigenberg, "The National Crime Survey and Rape: The Case of the Missing Question," *Justice Quarterly* 7:4 (December 1990).

42. David Johnston, "Survey Shows Number of Rapes Far Higher than Official Figures," *New York Times,* 24 April 1992, A9.

43. Gilbert, "The Phantom Epidemic of Sexual Assault," 64, 63, 65, 65.

44. See Gilbert, "Realities and Mythologies of Rape," 4–10.

45. Mary Koss, "Defending Date Rape," *Journal of Interpersonal Violence* 7:1 (March 1992), 124.

46. Virginia Matzek, "Students Protest Recent Article on Date Rape," *Daily Californian,* 7 June 1991, 1.

47. Roiphe, 52; Sommers, 212–13.

48. Mary Matalin, "Stop Whining!" *Newsweek,* 25 October 1993, 62.

49. Roiphe, 54, 55, 59.

50. Neil Gilbert, "Was It Rape?" *American Enterprise,* September 1994, 75.

51. Barbara Sullivan, "The Victim Trap," *Chicago Tribune,* 14 October 1993, sec. 5, p. 1.

52. Roiphe, 79.

53. John Leo, *Two Steps ahead of the Thought Police* (New York: Simon & Schuster, 1994), 235.

54. Jon Weiner, "'Rape by Innuendo' at Swarthmore," *Nation,* 20 January 1992, 44.

55. Wiener, "Rape by Innuendo." 45.

56. Nancy Gibbs, "When Is It Rape?" *Time,* 3 June 1991, 49.

57. Wiener, "'Rape by Innuendo,'" 45–46. In 1992, *Campus* reported that the definition of rape "has been expanded to include, as a Swarthmore College training manual describes, the 'spectrum of incidents and behaviors ranging from crimes legally defined as rape to verbal harassment and inappropriate innuendo'"; see Roger Landry, "The Politics of Rape," *Campus,* Winter 1992, 14.

58. Wiener, "'Rape by Innuendo,'" 47.

9

College Campuses
Need Antirape Policies
to Combat Date Rape

Bonnie Pfister

Bonnie Pfister is a freelance journalist living in New York City.

Policymakers and student activists have become more aware of the need for antirape programs to help prevent date rape and other forms of sexual violence on college campuses. Such programs may include detailed sexual consent policies, rape awareness and prevention workshops, stronger measures against acquaintance rape, and required sexual assault education for men and women. Since many students are unclear about what constitutes rape or how to respond to sexual assault, campuses must establish clear antirape policies.

What's an activist to do when everyone from George Will to "Saturday Night Live" satirizes your work and accuses you of infantilizing women and taking the fun out of sex?

"I find it exciting," says Jodi Gold, coordinator of STAAR, Students Together Against Acquaintance Rape at the University of Pennsylvania in Philadelphia. "You don't get a backlash until you've ruffled some feathers. It means we've really pushed the envelope and things are happening."

Fairer rules for sexual liaisons

The backlash has all but obscured the radical importance of student efforts to develop new—fairer—rules for sexual liaisons. The emerging new code includes the apparently controversial idea that potential lovers should *ask* before foisting sexual attention on their partners, and that partners should clearly *answer* "yes" or "no." In other words: people should communicate about their desires before making love, rather than waiting to be "swept away" by overwhelming passion.

While a deadpan legalistic approach to sex is easy to ridicule, Jodi

From Bonnie Pfister, "Swept Awake! Negotiating Passion on Campus." Reprinted by permission of *On the Issues: The Progressive Women's Quarterly*, Spring 1994, copyrighted © by Choices Women's Medical Center, Inc. To subscribe to *On the Issues*, call 1-800-783-4903, M–F 9 a.m.–8 p.m.

Gold believes that the real reason media coverage of today's campus activism is so highly critical is that Americans are still scared silly by its sexual frankness—a frankness that today's generation of young people desperately need.

"Sexuality is perhaps the most defining issue for today's students," says Alan Guskin, president of Antioch College in Ohio for nine years, and a supporter of the often-mocked Sexual Offense Policy, the student-written rules for sexual conduct at the college, which have been in place since fall 1992.

"Men and women students come to the campus with a very different consciousness about sexuality," notes Dr. Guskin. "The women have learned they have a right to determine how their bodies are used, but many of the young men still think the central question is how to get women to do what they want." The best way to deal with the situation, says Guskin, is for women and men to learn to communicate with each other. "The policy gives no specific checklist or statements. But there is a sense of how you should behave."

The Antioch policy says verbal consent is needed before all sexual contact, and that consent is an on-going process that can be withdrawn at any time. Students who are sleeping or unconscious or incapacitated by alcohol or drugs are not considered capable of consent. The policy also defines offenses as unwanted touching, verbal harassment, and non-disclosure of sexually transmitted disease, including HIV, and defines punishments for violations of various parts of the policy. All students are required to attend an educational workshop on consent and sexual offense each academic year.

Guskin notes that the media swarming over the campus for two and a half months reporting on the controversial policy accomplished more student education on the issue than the college's past several years of effort.

The Antioch policy

The policy emerged when thirty feminists disrupted a campus government meeting in November, 1990, demanding institutional rules to deal with rape, says Bethany Saltman, Antioch '93 and member of the original group, the Womyn of Antioch. Even at this tiny (650 students in the fall of 1993) alternative college, the administration seemed to prefer to keep rape reports under wraps. Faced with vehement, relentless protest and a flurry of local news attention, the administration reluctantly accepted the feminists' demand to remove any accused perpetrator from campus within twenty-four hours of a reported rape. But the rule was adopted on the condition that a committee of concerned staff and students would work to retool the policy while the administration consulted lawyers about its constitutionality. Womyn of Antioch demanded the policy out of strength, not weakness, notes Saltman. "We get to say who touches us, and where."

The policy has been criticized as a return to the 1950s that disempowers women by viewing them as damsels in distress and spells the death of *amour*.

Perhaps the critics are upset because they're embarrassed, says Elizabeth Sullivan, Antioch '93, now of Seattle. "It's still very hard for people to be explicit about sexual intimacy. The policy limits certain options, such as casual, thoughtless sex, while encouraging other options, such as accountability, sexual equality, and living in a community with a reduced fear of harassment or coerced sex."

Sullivan notes that critics act as though, without this policy, there is no social context influencing student's interactions at all. "Most of us acquire a whole set of norms and attitudes before we become sexual with other people. We learn who is an acceptable partner, we learn unspoken codes of how to proceed, and we develop a set of expectations about what sex should be," says Sullivan. In an intentional community like Antioch, people can choose to restructure that context.

Some students from other campuses who have adopted the Antioch rules as their own don't understand what all the fuss is about. Matthew Mizel, a student at Stanford (CA), likens the current resistance to people's initial embarrassment about asking a partner to use a condom during the early years of the AIDS crisis. "Why do people feel asking is not romantic?" asks Mizel. "All it does is clarify things. For me, it's not a romantic situation until I know the woman is comfortable."

As a letter writer to *The New Yorker* noted, asking permission, as in— "may I kiss the hollow of your neck?"—does not have to be devoid of *amour*.

Students should be relieved to discard the old stereotypes that "masculine sexuality is dangerous, passionate, reckless, and that the woman is passive and just laying back there," according to Mizel.

Callie Cary, an Antioch spokeswoman, herself out of college for less than a decade, scoffs at the idea that the asking-before-you-touch policy infantilizes women. "The assumption that this policy is about women saying no to men is based on the idea that men initiate sex all the time. But I know there are men on this campus who feel the women are very aggressive."

Activism on other campuses

While Antioch's policy contains the most detailed rules for sexual correctness to date, feminist actions on a number of campuses have expanded from helping rape victims *after* the fact to including a preventive approach. These efforts by female—and male—students are cropping up at conservative, co-ed universities like Syracuse (NY) and Vanderbilt (TN), as well as traditionally liberal women's colleges, such as Barnard (NY) and Mount Holyoke (MA). Private schools such as Stanford and Duke (NC) Universities boast dynamic men's groups examining why men rape and striving to prevent it, while students at public Evergreen State (WA) and Rutgers University (NJ) are reaching out to local high school girls with educational programs. On black college campuses the emphasis is on how the negative depiction of women in rap music discourages fair treatment in the sexual arena.

Most student organizers express some reservations over Antioch's policy: some hate it, while others herald it as swinging the pendulum dramatically to the side of open communication about sex—so far, in fact, that they might not need to adopt such a radical approach at their own schools (phew!).

"I would love to address the Antioch policy, but from what I can gather from other people on our committee, it would be suicide for us to consider it here," says Melinda Lewis, a sophomore at Vanderbilt University in Nashville and president of Students For Women's Concerns. After speaking in spring 1992 with rape survivors who felt revictimized by the school's judicial system, Lewis resumed in the fall to push for a new sexual assault policy. Although she is sensitive to Katie Roiphe–inspired charges of "victim feminism," she counters that the term does not accurately describe the activism—or the problems—she sees around her.

At Lehigh University (PA), Jeanne Clery was robbed, sodomized and murdered in her dorm bed by a student she had never met. Jeanne's own actions that night—it is believed that she left her door unlocked for her roommate's convenience—made it clear that students are often shockingly oblivious to the dangers around them. At the time, in 1986, Lehigh students regularly propped open outside doors to allow friends to come and go easily. Lehigh had "studied" the security problem for eleven years but taken no action until after Jeanne's death, according to Lynda Getchis of Security on Campus, a group founded by Clery's parents.

Asking permission, as in—"may I kiss the hollow of your neck?"—does not have to be devoid of amour.

After this incident, then-freshman Congressman Jim Ramstad (R-MN) joined forces with Clery's parents and crafted the Campus Sexual Assault Victims Bill of Rights. Signed into law in 1990, it requires that all postsecondary schools that receive federal funding publish annual reports about crime statistics on campus, institute policies to deal with sexual assault and offer rape awareness educational programs.

For 1991, the first year statistics were collected, 2,300 American campuses reported 30 murders, 1,000 rapes, and more than 1,800 robberies, according to *The Chronicle of Higher Education*. Most campus crime (78%) is student-on-student. While the crime incidence on campus is lower than that of the country as a whole, student and parent perceptions of the campus as a safe haven make the crime levels seem more shocking.

There is much controversy about just how many women experience sexual assault at college—the figures range from a scary 1 in 25 to a horrifying 1 in 4. But even the smallest estimates amount to a large threat to women's safety.

So it's no wonder that student activists are increasingly pressing their colleges to own up to the reality of crime and to codify, in writing, the kind of campus they want. The demands usually include more stringent acquaintance rape policies and mandatory peer education for students of both genders.

In the past five years, student activists have increasingly focused on university policies, notes Claire Kaplan, sexual assault education coordinator at the University of Virginia. "This strategy can be construed as students asking for protection, but it is not a throwback to *in loco parentis*. The institution has a contract with the student—the same kind of contract that could result in a third party suit against employers or landlords who fail to provide adequate protection against crime on their premises."

Today's students are also coming of age in a litigious, capitalist culture and many adopt a consumerist creed: "I pay a lot of money to go to this school, I deserve to be protected from assault and, at the very least, informed of its incidence on campus."

Coming of age in the '90s

Today's young activists have a point of view so different from those of the 1960s and '70s that commentators have had difficulty making the connections. In the '60s it was college men who had their lives on the line with the threat of being drafted to serve in the unpopular war in Vietnam. But today it is the women, and threat of rape, that's the flashpoint.

And unlike the rebels of the '60s and '70s who were trying to tear down repressive rules, institutions and social establishments, the generation growing up in the no-rules '90s is striving to build up a foundation of acceptable personal conduct and institutionalized norms.

At Evergreen State College in Olympia, WA, the administration had spent two years, with no end in sight, developing an anti-rape protocol. In the spring of 1993, rage at slow adjudication of a rape charge boiled over into graffiti hits around campus. The scribblers named names and proclaimed, "Rape Me and I'll Kill You," said Nina Fischer, a member of the Rape Response Coalition. The university protocol went into effect last fall, and students plan to take their rape awareness workshops to local high schools this spring.

Students are often shockingly oblivious to the dangers around them.

Radical approaches are less popular at a school like North Carolina State University in Raleigh, says Brian Ammons, a founder of that school's REAL-Men (Rape Education and Active Leadership). Originally active as the male-involvement voice in crafting a campus sex offense protocol, Ammons formed the group to examine male socialization and responsibility in a rape culture. In fact, at NCSU, it was REAL-Men that organized fall 1993's Take Back the Night march. The resident women's group, Help, Education and Activism on Rape (HEAR-Women) developed out of that.

"In some ways it was easier for a group of men to come together to offer some legitimacy on the issue," Ammons says. "Women on our campus are afraid to speak up about a lot of things. The fear of being labeled a feminist and being alienated here is very real."

Melinda Lewis, an African American, is a sophomore at Vanderbilt and president of Students For Women's Concerns, a predominantly white feminist group. "People question my involvement," she says. "The rape issue is perceived as something with which only Anglo, middle-class women are concerned. But that's a misguided notion. Women of color are raped and assaulted much more frequency than Anglo women."

Jennifer Lipton, a Barnard College student involved in rewriting sexual offense policy for the Columbia-Barnard community amidst administrator recalcitrance, agrees that the perception of acquaintance rape as a "white women's issue" flies in the face of reality. At the rape crisis center at St. Luke's–Roosevelt Hospital nearby, where she is a volunteer, most of the survivors she sees are women of color, most very poor, some homeless. "Their concerns are very different," Lipton says. "If their perpetrator is also black, they wonder if they should report it to the police. They are very aware of the racism of the judicial system, and worried about what it will do to their own community if they turn in this man. They also know that, as poor black women, society doesn't really value what they say."

However, at many African American colleges, date rape is a significantly less prominent gender concern than how women are depicted in rap music and advertising, reports Dionne Lyne, a student at the all-women Spelman College in Atlanta and member of the new campus organization SISTERS (Sisters in Solidarity to Eradicate Sexism). There's also anger at the persistent reference to certain Pan-Hellenic parties as "Greek Freaks," because of the use of "freak" as a disparaging term depicting black women as nymphomaniacs.

"There is a silence on the issue, a sense of, 'Yeah, it happens but we really don't want to know about it.' It reinforces the [idea] that these things happen to bad women, and we're just going to assume that we are all striving to be Spelman women, who are finer than that," Lyne says.

Spelman and brother school Morehouse College frequently co-sponsor educational programs about acquaintance rape, but Lyne says many women get the sense that Morehouse men are lecturing them about the issue, as if the men don't have a thing or two of their own to learn about date rape. Morehouse organizations have frequently scheduled their programs on Spelman's campus rather than their own, and fill the room with women and just one or two men.

Thomas Prince, associate director of counseling at Morehouse, counters that there are numerous anti-rape programs on the men's campus for co-ed groups, but his description of them seemed to indicate upon whom the responsibility is placed.

"We cover the FBI statistics, . . . talk about the things that might be contributing to the rise of acquaintance rapes and what to do if it happens to you. [That is] . . . what women can do if they find themselves in that situation," Prince said.

Prince states that there is no student group specifically organizing around this problem at Morehouse, and felt the Antioch policy did not encompass the way African-American men and women communicate about sex. "The language used around African American males is different," Prince said. "They have their own way of communicating verbally."

Men against rape

Some male activists are just as disturbed as their female counterparts with men's penchants during educational programs, for doggedly questioning the technical definition of rape or assault, rather than focusing on the nature of sexual relationships themselves.

"It's always coming up: 'What if this happens? Is this rape? How about that—is that rape?'" said James Newell, a senior at Syracuse University and president of the five-year-old coed student group SCARED (Students Concerned About Rape Education). "Men feel victimized by groups like ours. But we are not a group that's against sex."

Examining male expectations of sex is one tactic used at Duke University in Durham, NC, by the four-year-old student group Men Acting for Change (MAC). Pornography as sex education for men is a focal point of at least one of the eight-session course on men and gender issues, a topic that precedes the class on rape, says Jason Schultz, a MAC cofounder who graduated in spring 1993.

The most progressive voices among college students are determined to rewrite the sexual code to fit the needs of their generation.

While most of the women activists interviewed praised the men's organizations that are working against sexual violence, many expressed reservations and some suspicions about token support from other men's groups. One woman who asked not to be named criticized a men's group on her campus whose sole pro-feminist action is an annual day-long wearing of white ribbons to signify opposition to sexual assault. "Frankly I think it's a very shallow and trivial way of responding," she said.

Kelly Wall, a founder of HEAR-Women at North Carolina State, expressed irritation that the most visible anti-rape presence on campus before HEAR was comprised of men.

The REAL-Men group is aware of the apparent irony of the situation. "We're very conscious of what our place is. We don't want to take over the issue, " Ammons says. Although his group does deal with "secondary survivors" (men who are grappling with their feelings about the rape of a lover, friend or relative), it is with some hesitation that they discuss the issues of male survivors of sexual offense.

Anti-rape activist Matthew Mizel at Stanford University says he sometimes feels his motivation questioned. Mizel founded Stanford Men's Collective in fall 1992 to discuss where rape comes from and how to stop it by examining men's own behavior. A talkative, outgoing senior easily recognized on campus by his long blond hair, Mizel says the praise he gets from women for his work generates curiosity and the occasional impression that he's doing it to "get laid."

"Men have asked if I'm trying to gain points with women and be some kind of super-heterosexual. . . . And some women have asked if I'm gay—as if there was no chance that I'm just a regular person who cares about this issue," Mizel said.

These young men make it clear that anti-rape work is not just a woman's thing, and that the most progressive voices among college students are determined to rewrite the sexual code to fit the needs of their generation.

And they agree that a rewrite is necessary. At the University of Virginia, Claire Kaplan described a seminar in which several fraternity men asserted: "When you get to a certain point during sex you can't stop," an attitude she thought had long since fallen to the wayside. "That's why the Antioch policy was created," she notes. "There is still the attitude—don't talk, just do."

10

Antirape Policies Are Ineffective

Camille Paglia

Camille Paglia is a professor of humanities at the University of the Arts in Philadelphia, Pennsylvania. She is also the author of Sexual Personae: Art and Decadence from Nefertiti to Emily Dickinson *and* Sex, Art, and American Culture, *from which this viewpoint is excerpted.*

Campus antirape policies do not prevent acquaintance rape. These policies, which are often promoted by feminist activists, lead women to believe that gender equality exists and that women should have the same freedoms as men. Such attitudes discount the realities of aggressive male sexuality and encourage women to participate in unsafe activities that include the risk of rape. To prevent date rape, women must become more self-aware and learn to avoid potentially dangerous situations.

Rape is an outrage that cannot be tolerated in civilized society. Yet feminism, which has waged a crusade for rape to be taken more seriously, has put young women in danger by hiding the truth about sex from them.

In dramatizing the pervasiveness of rape, feminists have told young women that before they have sex with a man, they must give consent as explicit as a legal contract's. In this way, young women have been convinced that they have been the victims of rape. On elite campuses in the Northeast and on the West Coast, they have held consciousness-raising sessions, petitioned administrations, demanded inquests. At Brown University, outraged, panicky "victims" have scrawled the names of alleged attackers on the walls of women's rest rooms. What marital rape was to the Seventies, "date rape" is to the Nineties.

The incidence and seriousness of rape do not require this kind of exaggeration. Real acquaintance rape is nothing new. It has been a horrible problem for women for all of recorded history. Once fathers and brothers protected women from rape. Once the penalty for rape was death. I come from a fierce Italian tradition where, not so long ago in the motherland, a rapist would end up knifed, castrated, and hung out to dry.

But the old clans and small rural communities have broken down. In our cities, on our campuses far from home, young women are vulnerable and defenseless. Feminism has not prepared them for this. Feminism keeps saying the sexes are the same. It keeps telling women they can do anything, go anywhere, say anything, wear anything. No, they can't. Women will always be in sexual danger.

[Feminism] keeps telling women they can do anything, go anywhere, say anything, wear anything. No, they can't. Women will always be in sexual danger.

One of my male students recently slept overnight with a friend in a passageway of the Great Pyramid in Egypt. He described the moon and sand, the ancient silence and eerie echoes. I will never experience that. I am a woman. I am not stupid enough to believe I could ever be safe there. There is a world of solitary adventure I will never have. Women have always known these somber truths. But feminism, with its pie-in-the-sky fantasies about the perfect world, keeps young women from seeing life as it is.

Humans cannot change sexual realities

We must remedy social injustice whenever we can. But there are some things we cannot change. There are sexual differences that are based in biology. Academic feminism is lost in a fog of social constructionism. It believes we are totally the product of our environment. This idea was invented by [French philosopher Jean-Jacques] Rousseau. He was wrong. Emboldened by dumb French language theory, academic feminists repeat the same hollow slogans over and over to each other. Their view of sex is naïve and prudish. Leaving sex to the feminists is like letting your dog vacation at the taxidermist's.

The sexes are at war. Men must struggle for identity against the overwhelming power of their mothers. Women have menstruation to tell them they are women. Men must do or risk something to be men. Men become masculine only when other men say they are. Having sex with a woman is one way a boy becomes a man.

College men are at their hormonal peak. They have just left their mothers and are questing for their male identity. In groups, they are dangerous. A woman going to a fraternity party is walking into Testosterone Flats, full of prickly cacti and blazing guns. If she goes, she should be armed with resolute alertness. She should arrive with girlfriends and leave with them. A girl who lets herself get dead drunk at a fraternity party is a fool. A girl who goes upstairs alone with a brother at a fraternity party is an idiot. Feminists call this "blaming the victim." I call it common sense.

For a decade, feminists have drilled their disciples to say, "Rape is a crime of violence but not of sex." This sugar-coated Shirley Temple nonsense has exposed young women to disaster. Misled by feminism, they do not expect rape from the nice boys from good homes who sit next to them in class.

Aggression and eroticism are deeply intertwined. Hunt, pursuit, and capture are biologically programmed into male sexuality. Generation after generation, men must be educated, refined, and ethically persuaded away from their tendency toward anarchy and brutishness. Society is not the enemy, as feminism ignorantly claims. Society is woman's protection against rape. Feminism, with its solemn Carry Nation repressiveness, does not see what is for men the eroticism or fun element in rape, especially the wild, infectious delirium of gang rape. Women who do not understand rape cannot defend themselves against it.

The date-rape controversy shows feminism hitting the wall of its own broken promises. The women of my Sixties generation were the first respectable girls in history to swear like sailors, get drunk, stay out all night—in short, to act like men. We sought total sexual freedom and equality. But as time passed, we woke up to cold reality. The old double standard protected women. When anything goes, it's women who lose.

Today's young women don't know what they want. They see that feminism has not brought sexual happiness. The theatrics of public rage over date rape are their way of restoring the old sexual rules that were shattered by my generation. Because nothing about the sexes has really changed. The comic film *Where the Boys Are* (1960), the ultimate expression of Fifties man-chasing, still speaks directly to our time. It shows smart, lively women skillfully anticipating and fending off the dozens of strategies with which horny men try to get them into bed. The agonizing date-rape subplot and climax are brilliantly done. The victim, Yvette Mimieux, makes mistake after mistake, obvious to the other girls. She allows herself to be lured away from her girlfriends and into isolation with boys whose character and intentions she misreads. *Where the Boys Are* tells the truth. It shows courtship as a dangerous game in which the signals are not verbal but subliminal.

The only solution to date rape is female self-awareness and self-control.

Neither militant feminism, which is obsessed with politically correct language, nor academic feminism, which believes that knowledge and experience are "constituted by" language, can understand preverbal or nonverbal communication. Feminism, focusing on sexual politics, cannot see that sex exists in and through the body. Sexual desire and arousal cannot be fully translated into verbal terms. This is why men and women misunderstand each other.

Trying to remake the future, feminism cut itself off from sexual history. It discarded and suppressed the sexual myths of literature, art, and religion. Those myths show us the turbulence, the mysteries and passions of sex. In mythology we see men's sexual anxiety, their fear of woman's dominance. Much sexual violence is rooted in men's sense of psychological weakness toward women. It takes many men to deal with one woman. Woman's voracity is a persistent motif. Clara Bow, it was rumored, took on the USC [University of Southern California] football team on weekends. Marilyn Monroe, singing "Diamonds Are a Girl's Best Friend," rules a conga line of men in tuxes. Half-clad Cher, in the video for "If I Could Turn Back Time," deranges a battleship of screaming sailors and straddles a pink-lit cannon. Feminism, coveting social power, is blind to woman's cosmic sexual power.

Women are responsible for preventing rape

To understand rape, you must study the past. There never was and never will be sexual harmony. Every woman must take personal responsibility for her sexuality, which is nature's red flame. She must be prudent and cautious about where she goes and with whom. When she makes a mistake, she must accept the consequences and, through self-criticism, resolve never to make that mistake again. Running to Mommy and Daddy on the campus grievance committee is unworthy of strong women. Posting lists of guilty men in the toilet is cowardly, infantile stuff.

The Italian philosophy of life espouses high-energy confrontation. A male student makes a vulgar remark about your breasts? Don't slink off to whimper and simper with the campus shrinking violets. Deal with it. On the spot. Say, "Shut up, you jerk! And crawl back to the barnyard where you belong!" In general, women who project this take-charge attitude toward life get harassed less often. I see too many dopey, immature, self-pitying women walking around like melting sticks of butter. It's the Yvette Mimieux syndrome: make me happy. And listen to me weep when I'm not.

The date-rape debate is already smothering in propaganda churned out by the expensive Northeastern colleges and universities, with their overconcentration of boring, uptight academic feminists and spoiled, affluent students. Beware of the deep manipulativeness of rich students who were neglected by their parents. They love to turn the campus into hysterical psychodramas of sexual transgression, followed by assertions of parental authority and concern. And don't look for sexual enlightenment from academe, which spews out mountains of books but never looks at life directly.

As a fan of football and rock music, I see in the simple, swaggering masculinity of the jock and in the noisy posturing of the heavy-metal guitarist certain fundamental, unchanging truths about sex. Masculinity is aggressive, unstable, combustible. It is also the most creative cultural force in history. Women must reorient themselves toward the elemental powers of sex, which can strengthen or destroy.

The only solution to date rape is female self-awareness and self-control. A woman's number one line of defense is herself. When a real rape occurs, she should report it to the police. Complaining to college committees because the courts "take too long" is ridiculous. College administrations are not a branch of the judiciary. They are not equipped or trained for legal inquiry. Colleges must alert incoming students to the problems and dangers of adulthood. Then colleges must stand back and get out of the sex game.

Organizations to Contact

The editors have compiled the following list of organizations concerned with the issues debated in this book. The descriptions are derived from materials provided by the organizations themselves. All have publications or information available for interested readers. The list was compiled on the date of publication of the present volume; names, addresses, phone and fax numbers, and e-mail and Internet addresses may change. Be aware that many organizations take several weeks or longer to respond to inquiries, so allow as much time as possible.

Campus Violence Prevention Center
Towson State University
Towson, MD 21204-7097
(410) 830-2178

This research center conducts national surveys of such campus issues as date rape, campus violence, and alcohol consumption. It has two publications, *Responding to Violence on Campus,* a sourcebook of papers presented at various conferences, and *The Links Among Alcohol, Drugs, and Crime on American College Campuses,* a book based on national surveys.

Center for the Prevention of Sexual and Domestic Violence (CPSDV)
936 N. 34th St., Suite 200
Seattle, WA 98103
(206) 634-1903
fax: (206) 634-0115
e-mail: cpsdv@cpsdv.com
Internet: http://www.cpsdv.org

The CPSDV is an educational resource center that works with both religious and secular communities throughout the United States and Canada to address the issues of sexual abuse and domestic violence. The center offers workshops concerning sexual misconduct by clergy, spouse abuse, child sexual abuse, rape, and pornography. Materials available from the CPSDV include the quarterly newsletter *Working Together* and the books *Sexual Abuse Prevention: A Course of Study for Teenagers, Violence Against Women and Children,* and *Sexual Violence: The Unmentionable Sin.*

Center for Women Policy Studies (CWPS)
1211 Connecticut Ave. NW, Suite 312
Washington, DC 20036
(202) 872-1770
fax: (202) 296-8962
e-mail: cwpsx@aol.com

The CWPS is an independent feminist policy research and advocacy institution established in 1972. The center studies policies affecting the social, legal, health, and economic status of women. It publishes the booklets *Campus Gang Rape* and *Campus Sexual Harassment,* as well as reports on a variety of topics related to women's equality and empowerment, including sexual harassment, campus rape, and violence against women.

National Association of College and University Attorneys
1 Dupont Circle, Suite 620
Washington, DC 20036
(202) 833-8390
fax: (202) 296-8379
e-mail: nacua@nacua.org
Internet: http://www.nacua.org

The association represents approximately fourteen hundred U.S. and Canadian colleges and universities in legal matters. It compiles and distributes legal decisions, opinions, and other writings and information on legal problems affecting colleges and universities. Publications include *Acquaintance Rape on Campus: A Model for Institutional Response* and *Crime on Campus*.

National Center on Addiction and Substance Abuse (CASA)
Columbia University
152 W. 57th St., 12th Fl.
New York, NY 10019
(212) 841-5200
fax: (212) 956-8020
Internet: http://www.casacolumbia.org

The center conducts research related to substance abuse and addiction. In its June 1994 report, *Rethinking Rites of Passage: Substance Abuse on America's Campuses,* a panel found that 90 percent of all reported campus rapes take place when the assailant or victim is using alcohol.

National Coalition of Free Men
PO Box 129
Manhasset, NY 11030
(516) 482-6378
e-mail: information@ncfm.org
Internet: http://www.ncfm.org

The coalition's members include men seeking "a fair and balanced perspective on gender issues." The organization promotes men's legal rights in issues such as false accusation of rape, sexual harassment, and sexual abuse. It conducts research, sponsors educational programs, maintains a database on men's issues, and publishes the bimonthly *Transitions*.

National Criminal Justice Reference Service (NCJRS)
PO Box 6000
Rockville, MD 20849-6000
(310) 519-5063
e-mail: askncjrs@ncjrs.org
Internet: http://www.ncjrs.org

In 1972 the National Institute of Justice, the research and development agency of the U.S. Department of Justice, established the NCJRS as its clearinghouse. It provides studies and statistics on child rape victims, child victimizers, and violence against women. Among its publications are the reports "The Criminal Justice and Community Response to Rape" and "When the Victim Is a Child."

NOW Legal Defense and Education Fund
99 Hudson St.
New York, NY 10013
(212) 925-6635
fax: (212) 226-1066
Internet: http://www.nowldef.org

The NOW Legal Defense and Education Fund is a branch of the National Organization for Women (NOW). It provides legal referrals and conducts research on a broad range of issues concerning women and the law. It offers a comprehensive list of publications, including testimony on sexual harassment, books, articles, reports, and briefs. The fund offers legal resource kits pertaining to a variety of issues, including violence against women.

Office for Victims of Crime Resource Center
810 Seventh St. NW
Washington, DC 20531
(800) 627-6872
Internet: http://www.ojp.usdoj.gov/ovc

Established in 1983 by the U.S. Department of Justice's Office for Victims of Crime, the resource center is a primary source of information regarding victim-related issues. It answers questions by using national and regional statistics, research findings, and a network of victim advocates and organizations. The center distributes all Office of Justice Programs (OJP) publications, including *Female Victims of Violent Crime* and *Sexual Assault: An Overview*.

People Against Rape (PAR)
PO Box 5876
Naperville, IL 60567
(800) 877-7252
e-mail: Personal_Empowerment_Programs@msn.com

People Against Rape primarily seeks to help teens and children avoid becoming the victims of sexual assault and rape by providing instruction in the basic principles of self-defense. PAR further promotes self-esteem and motivation of teens and college students through educational programs. Publications include the books *Defend: Preventing Date Rape and Other Sexual Assaults* and *Sexual Assault: How to Defend Yourself*.

Sex Information and Education Council of the U.S. (SIECUS)
130 W. 42nd St., Suite 350
New York, NY 10036-7802
(212) 819-9770
fax: (212) 819-9776
e-mail: siecus@siecus.org
Internet: http://www.siecus.org

SIECUS is a clearinghouse for information on sexuality, with a special interest in sex education. It publishes sex education curricula, the bimonthly newsletter *SIECUS Report,* and fact sheets on sex education issues. Its articles, bibliographies, and book reviews often address the role of sex education in identifying, reducing, and preventing sexual violence.

Survivor Connections
52 Lyndon Rd.
Cranston, RI 02905-1121
(401) 941-2548

Survivor Connections is an activist organization for survivors of sexual assault. It provides referrals to attorneys, therapists, and peer support groups. The organization also seeks to educate the public about legislation affecting survivors and encourages criminal prosecution and civil claims against perpetrators. A quarterly newspaper, the *Survivor Activist,* is available to the general public.

Bibliography

Books

Julie A. Allison and Lawrence S. Wrightsman
Rape: The Misunderstood Crime. Newbury Park, CA: Sage Publications, 1993.

Sandra Lipsitz Bem
The Lenses of Gender: Transforming the Debate on Sexual Inequality. New Haven, CT: Yale University Press, 1993.

Raquel Kennedy Bergen
Wife Rape: Understanding the Response of Survivors and Service Providers. Thousand Oaks, CA: Sage Publications, 1996.

Carol Bohmer and Andrea Parrot
Sexual Assault on Campus: The Problem and the Solution. New York: Lexington Books, 1993.

Emilie Buchwald, Pamela Fletcher, and Martha Roth, eds.
Transforming a Rape Culture. Minneapolis: Milkweed Editions, 1993.

David M. Buss and Neil M. Malamuth
Sex, Power, Conflict: Evolutionary and Feminist Perspectives. New York: Oxford University Press, 1996.

Leslie Francis, ed.
Date Rape: Feminism, Philosophy, and the Law. University Park: Pennsylvania State University Press, 1996.

Rus Ervin Funk
Stopping Rape: A Challenge for Men. Philadelphia: New Society Publishers, 1995.

Illinois Coalition Against Sexual Abuse
Sexual Violence: Facts and Statistics. Springfield, IL: The Coalition, 1993.

Mary P. Koss and Mary R. Harvey
The Rape Victim: Clinical and Community Interventions. Newbury Park, CA: Sage Publications, 1991.

Mary P. Koss et al.
No Safe Haven: Male Violence Against Women at Home, at Work, and in the Community. Washington, DC: American Psychological Association, 1994.

Nan Bauer Maglin and Donna Perry, eds.
"Bad Girls"/ "Good Girls": Women, Sex, and Power in the Nineties. New Brunswick, NJ: Rutgers University Press, 1996.

Nancy A. Matthews
Confronting Rape: The Feminist Anti-Rape Movement and the State. New York: Routledge, 1994.

Camille Paglia
Sex, Art, and American Culture: Essays. New York: Vintage Books, 1992.

Katie Roiphe
The Morning After: Sex, Fear, and Feminism on Campus. New York: New York University Press, 1996.

Peggy Reeves Sanday
A Woman Scorned: Acquaintance Rape on Trial. New York: Doubleday, 1996.

Martin D. Schwartz and Walter S. DeKeseredy	*Sexual Assault on the College Campus: The Role of Male Peer Support.* Thousand Oaks, CA: Sage Publications, 1997.
Christina Hoff Sommers	*Who Stole Feminism?: How Women Have Betrayed Women.* New York: Simon & Schuster, 1994.
Adele M. Stan	*Debating Sexual Correctness: Pornography, Sexual Harassment, Date Rape, and the Politics of Sexual Equality.* New York: Dell, 1995.
Robin Warshaw	*I Never Called It Rape: The* Ms. *Report on Recognizing, Fighting, and Surviving Date and Acquaintance Rape.* New York: HarperPerennial, 1994.
Vernon R. Wiehe and Ann L. Richards	*Intimate Betrayal: Understanding and Responding to the Trauma of Acquaintance Rape.* Thousand Oaks, CA: Sage Publications, 1995.

Periodicals

Kathryn Abrams	"Songs of Innocence and Experience: Dominance Feminism in the University," *Yale Law Journal,* April 1994.
Nelson W. Aldrich Jr.	"How to Avoid Date Rape," *Wilson Quarterly,* Spring 1994.
Ronet Bachman and Raymond Paternoster	"A Contemporary Look at the Effects of Rape Law Reform: How Far Have We Really Come?" *Journal of Criminal Law & Criminology,* vol. 84, no. 3, 1993.
Margaret D. Bonilla	"Cultural Assault: What Feminists Are Doing to Rape Ought to Be a Crime," *Policy Review,* Fall 1993.
Sarah Crichton	"Sexual Correctness: Has It Gone Too Far?" *Newsweek,* October 25, 1993.
Barbara Ehrenreich	"Wartime in the Barracks: Here's a Radical Solution to Ending the Harassment of Women in the Military," *Time,* December 2, 1996.
Susan Faludi	"Whose Hype? Date-Rape Revisionists Attack the Victim Mind-Set," *Newsweek,* October 25, 1993.
Eric Felten	"Sex and the Single Soldier," *National Review,* April 7, 1997.
Neil Gilbert	"Miscounting Social Ills," *Society,* March/April 1994.
Jeff Giles with Stanley Holmes	"There's a Time for Talk, and a Time for Action," *Newsweek,* March 7, 1994.
Peter Hellman	"Crying Rape: The Politics of Date Rape on Campus," *New York,* March 8, 1993.
Liz Holtzman and Alice Vachss	"Let's Get Tough On Rape," *On the Issues,* Summer 1994.
Carol Iannone	"Sex and the Feminists," *Commentary,* September 1993.

Ida M. Johnson and Robert T. Sigler — "Forced Sexual Intercourse on Campus: Crime or Offensive Behavior?" *Journal of Contemporary Criminal Justice*, vol. 12, no.1, February 1996. Available from the Department of Criminal Justice, California State University, Long Beach, 1250 Bellflower Blvd., Long Beach, CA 90840.

Cindi Leive — "Women Right Now: The Dangerous Truth About Acquaintance Rape," *Glamour*, June 1993.

Linda Marsa — "The New Date-Rape Drug," *Glamour*, November 1997.

Wendy McElroy — "The Unfair Sex?" *National Review*, May 1, 1995.

Lynn Hecht Schafran — "Rape Is Still Underreported," *New York Times*, August 26, 1995.

Bruce Shapiro — "Rape's Defenders," *Nation*, July 1, 1996.

Del Thiessen and Robert K. Young — "Investigating Sexual Coercion," *Society*, March/April 1994.

Gregory L. Vistica — "Rape in the Ranks," *Newsweek*, November 25, 1996.

Jennifer Wolff — "Sex by the Rules," *Glamour*, May 1994.

Index